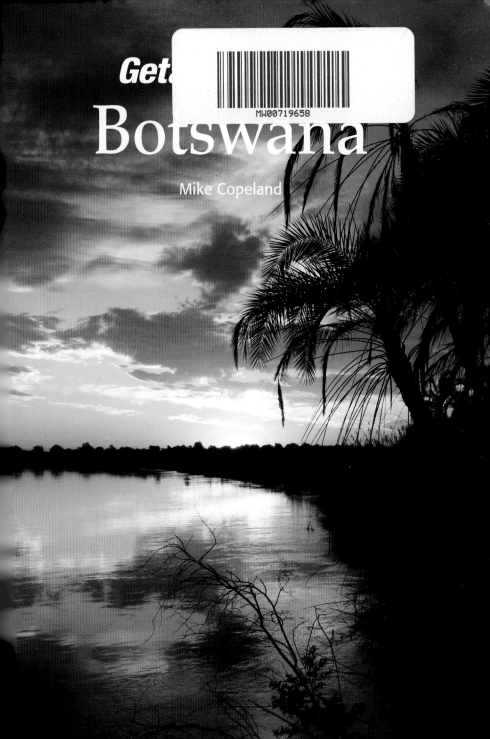

Geta

Botswana

Mike Copeland

SUNBIRD
PUBLISHERS

First published in 2009
Second edition in 2010

Sunbird Publishers (Pty) Ltd
PO Box 6836, Roggebaai, Cape Town, 8012
www.sunbirdpublishers.co.za

Registration number: 1984\003543\07

Publisher Ceri Prenter
Editor David Bristow
Design and typeset Marisa Steyn
Proofreader Kathleen Sutton
Cartography by John Hall
Index Josephine Bestic

Reproduction by Resolution Colour, Cape Town
Printed by Tien Wah Press (Pte), Singapore

ISBN 978-1-920289-31-7

FRONT COVER: Mekoro in the Delta; 4x4 trail, Kgalagadi Park; leopard in acacia, Moremi;
river accommodation in Francistown. BACK COVER: The author on the Panhandle.
TITLE PAGE: Sunset on Chobe. OPPOSITE: Kalahari meerkat sentinel.

Acknowledgements

I needed all the help and assistance I could get when writing a guide-book like this and, in particular, I would like to thank: Peter from Lodges of Botswana, Judy with Haina Safari Lodge, Garry of Okavango Riverboats, Neeltjie at Grasslands Safaris, Kabelo with Cresta Thapama Hotel, Sharon at Kubu Lodge, David from the Old Bridge Backpackers, Paula of Planet Baobab, Hendrik from Mokolodi Backpackers, Linda of Stevensford Game Reserve, Cynthia with Lehututu Lodge.

At Sunbird, publisher Ceri, David my editor, John for the maps and Anthony for his kindness at Toyota. Pats was, as always, my partner and travelling-companion on all our trips, assisting with notes and in a thousand other ways. And to all the people of Botswana who were so friendly and helpful and will always know more about their country than me, 'Pula!'

Mike Copeland
Paarl, May 2010

I proudly dedicate this book to Murray. May he grow to love Africa as much as his grandfather does.

Contents

MAP KEY AND REFERENCES

National route	⊕	Medical centre/hospital	Ⓘ	Restaurant/bar
Main route	⚠	Memorial/statue		Road, main route
Secondary route (4x4)	🏛	Monument building		Road
4x4 route	Ⓟ	Parking	▦	Shops
Lodge/accommodation	✳	Place of interest	📖	Library
Camping	Ⓦ	Place of worship	ℹ	Information
Garage, petrol/diesel	✵	Police station	🛏	Accommodation
Airport/airfield	Ⓑ	Bus terminus	Train station

This sandy track in the Ghanzi district of the Kalahari leads to the end of the rainbow.

A sundowner cruise on the Chobe River offers tourists sightings of game, birds and, of course, the sunset. The river separates Botswana and Namibia — but not without tensions.

HOW TO USE THIS BOOK

The first 10 chapters of this book are filled with information about Botswana, its history, people and natural environment, with notes on planning a trip, getting to your destination, staying safe and other practical aspects of travelling around the country. It is, from a people point of view, one of the safest places you'll find, in Africa anyway. However, on the wildlife side, from time to time tourists have lost their lives to – usually through carelessness it must be stressed – lions and crocodiles. The game reserves are very wild indeed so anyone not completely familiar with the African bush should be as circumspect as possible. Some of the suggestions and recommended equipment are applicable only for the wilder parts of the country and should not be necessary if you are staying in and around the larger towns. The last 9 chapters explore and describe Botswana town by town, region by region, starting with Gaborone and working around the country in an anticlockwise direction.

This guide can be used to plan a trip to, or travel throughout Botswana, on-road or off-road, either with your own vehicle, a hired one or even public transport. One of the best trips of my life, so far, was to travel from Cape Town to Cairo entirely on public transport. Road conditions and fuel availability, accommodation and food – it's all there. Botswana is so vast and its sights so spread out there is no single, ideal route through the country: choose your own route and then work your way through the applicable area chapters.

Prices are quoted in Botswanan pula (P). Prices are those charged to non-residents: residents and citizens sometimes pay substantially less, especially in game reserves. All accommodation prices given, unless otherwise stated, are assumed to be for one person for one night (which, in the case of most safari lodges, implies sharing a double room).

GPS co-ordinates are expressed in degrees, minutes and decimal fractions, while the datum setting used is WGS 84 (not Cape). Local telephone numbers are listed as you would dial them from within Botswana. All other foreign numbers, including South African, are preceded by the international and area dialing codes.

Introduction

The Call of the Wild is loud and clear in Botswana – it roars and bellows across the open spaces of this vast, almost flat country. There are not many countries left on our planet that have more than a fair share of pre-human-era fauna preserved into our modern age, and where they roam so widely and freely. Fortunate is the traveller who answers the call and experiences what Botswana has to offer. The adrenaline rush of predators in camp at night, of battering your vehicle through deep sand and water or mud, sipping sundowners while watching the sky turn red with the silhouettes of elephants drinking nearby, or just enjoying the silence and solitude of the salt pans: this is Botswana.

But it's a country you need to be prepared and equipped for. To draw the most out of your trip, to be able to get where you want to go and do what you want to do, it is necessary to plan and prepare carefully. As welcoming and beautiful as the country is, it can bite. There are wilderness areas where you will receive no backup or assistance if broken down; hot, waterless wastes where dehydration and death are a possibility, and always the wild animals – animals that can attack, trample and maul if they get the chance. So prepare yourself, your vehicle and equipment and, when you arrive home safely after the trip of a lifetime, know it was all worth it.

I must admit, my first trip to Botswana was with a young wife and babies in an ill-prepared VW Kombi that didn't even last the trip – we returned home by train. But it was another one of the memorable trips of my life and it started my long love affair with the country. My wisdom from this is to rather go ill-prepared than not go at all, as long as your head is prepared!

Maybe you are lucky enough to have included Botswana in a longer trip, taking in other southern African countries or even a cross-Africa trip. If so, I hope you have copies of my other guidebooks in this series: Cape to Cairo, Mozambique and Namibia. And I'm always keen to hear about your trips and offer assistance where I can. For this, or if you have any other information that might be useful for updating this book, please contact me on mcopeland@telkomsa.net.

BOTSWANA'S FLAG

The Botswana flag was officially unveiled at independence (it was previously a protectorate of Great Britain) on 30 September, 1966. The colours on the flag correspond to those on the national coat of arms: the blue represents water – this arid country's most prized resource; the white-black-white bands depict the pluralist nature of the society, as well as racial harmony. The inspiration are the stripes of the zebra, the national animal.

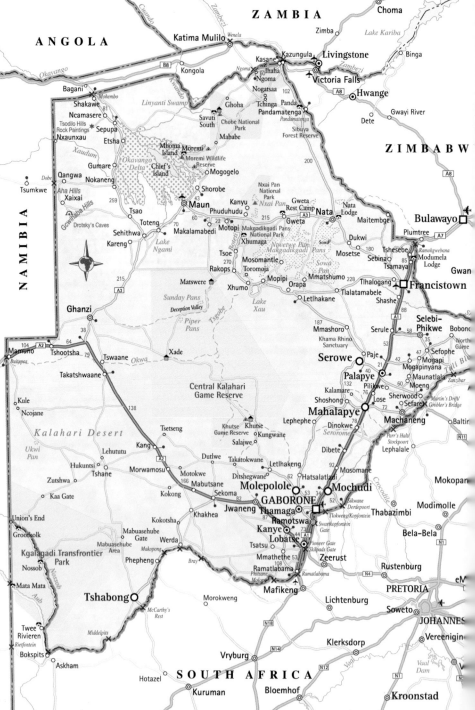

BOTSWANA

Facts, figures and highlights

1

Botswana is a large country with a small population, a good income mainly from diamonds and a stable, democratic government. There is lots to see and do, a good climate and a strong currency.

The serpentine channels and reed beds of the Okavango Delta are best comprehended from the air. It is an ever-changing 'land of water'.

An anomaly to many first-time, especially overseas, visitors is that the vast majority of the country is arid, dusty – what you might call 'empty' – and seemingly inhabited by dirt-poor stock farmers. Even quite recently the head of the country's central bank was quoted saying his dream was to retire to a cattle station in the 'bush'; in other words a typical rural cattle-farming village. Despite its economic development over the past 25 years, the majority of Batswana regard cattle as the most important economic possession and pretty much every family has or dreams of running a cattle station in the bush.

However, if you want to get a better grasp of modern, urban Botswana – and be mightily entertained along the way – you can do no better than to read the sagas of Botswana's number one literary icon. Scottish writer Alexander McCall Smith has entertained millions with his best-selling series of novels about engaging and resourceful Precious Ramotswe and her No. 1 Ladies' Detective Agency. It's empathetic comedy, detective story-telling and social comment in one rollicking package.

Size

Botswana is a big, chunky, landlocked country of just over 581 000 square kilometres nestled in the heart of southern Africa. At roughly the same size as France, Texas or Kenya, it is surrounded by neighbours Namibia (824 000 sq km), Angola (1 246 000 sq km), Zambia (752 000 sq km), Zimbabwe (390 000 sq km) and South Africa (1 221 000 sq km). The Tropic of Capricorn passes through the country just south of Mahalapye, which puts roughly two-thirds of the country in the tropics. Some 80 % of the country is covered by the Kalahari sand ecosystem, while most of the population is settled in the relatively more fertile extreme east and south-east.

Topography

With the majority of the country lying at an elevation of between 950 and 1 250 m, Botswana is as flat as you can imagine. The eastern fringe of the country has some sandstone and granite hills (koppies really) and this slightly higher topography drains into the Limpopo River. Otherwise Botswana is a vast basin covered in a mantle of geologically recent aoelian, or wind-carried, sands more than a

thousand metres deep at its centre. In the north it lies across an unstable geological belt. Frequent movements of the earth's crust play a significant role in determining that part of the country's hydrology. The centre is a dry, sandy expanse of low dunes punctuated by rare rocky outcrops such as Tsodilo Hills and Aha Hills. The vast salt pans of Makgadikgadi, Ntwetwe and Sowa have formed in the north-centre of the country and the most famous feature in the country, the Okavango Delta, fans out in the far north-centre. This unique freshwater delta is formed as the Okavango River flows down from the wet highlands of Angola and runs out of a fall in elevation – it has nowhere to go but spreads out in channels and lagoons of the delta and eventually evaporates or drains into the warm sands of the Kalahari.

In previous times the Okavango River was captured by the Zambezi drainage system but crustal movements, or earthquakes, altered the lie of the land. This sent the Okavango and related channels flowing southwards into the sand basin from which there is no outlet. The pans referred to above were once part of a huge inland sea, the high dunes that mark its ancient shoreline can best be seen along the route between Moremi and Savuti. Even today, earthquakes play a role in the landscape: since the first records by European travellers, water courses such as the Savuti Channel and Selinda Spillway have been witnessed to flow, stop flowing, and even change direction. This ancient mystery was unlocked only recently and today the wayward and often erratic flow of the various water channels

After rain the road across the pans to Baines' Baobabs can be muddy and treacherous.

Money, money, money! Botswana's currency is the pula, which means rain in Setswana.

that make up the greater Okavango system can be traced to seismic events in the area. Sometimes Lake Ngami is full, other times empty, depending on whether geological events dictate that the Botete River flows out of the Delta to the south, or not. It is an unusually busy area geologically, but all the action happens deep underground and is cushioned by that deep sand mantle. Partly this fickle geology and partly the general lack of surface water have dictated the slow way of life and development in the country.

The highest point in Botswana is the Tsodilo Hills at 1 489 m, while the lowest point is 513 m at the confluence of the Shashe and Limpopo rivers where Botswana, South Africa and Zimbabwe meet.

Climate

For a country that lies mainly in the tropics, Botswana is surprisingly hot and dry. It's often called a desert, but in fact is classified as arid savanna (sparse, sweet grasses with scattered trees). A true desert has an average annual rainfall of less than 250 mm, while Botswana's average is around 450 mm. Rains fall mainly in summer, between October and March, with the lowest falls in the south-west Kalahari region and the highest in the north-east around the Chobe River. During summer, average daytime temperatures hover around 37°C, while winter temperatures are a good 10°C lower and can drop below freezing at night. In the central Kalahari winter night-time temperatures as low as -12°C have been recorded, but the days are generally warm. (See pages 50 to 51 for clothing and personal gear.)

Cities and towns

With a small population spread over a large area, don't expect to find many big cities. The capital, Gaborone, is the largest but has fewer than 250 000 inhabitants. 'Gabs' is a pleasant, modern city with a good road system, shops, accommodation and infrastructure. Situated in the south-east of the country it is close to and has strong links with South Africa. Francistown is the second-largest but oldest modern town in Botswana. Situated in the north-east, it is an important crossroads to countries in the north, and Maun and the Delta to the west. It is also close to the Zimbabwean border and is an important railhead. Although Maun is a compact little town, it is the safari capital of Botswana and the jumping-off point for the Delta. Developing fast, it has good shops and a busy international airport. From there, small aircraft supply the many safari lodges across Ngamiland, the northern province.

Lobatse in the south-east is an important beef processing centre, linked to Ghanzi in the west-centre where large-scale cattle ranching prevails. Botswana is an important supplier of beef to the European community, and foot-and-mouth disease control is rigid. You should not attempt to take meat into the country, as it is likely to be confiscated at the border or one of the disease-control gates. Kasane is in the far north-east, on the Chobe River and borders with Namibia's eastern Caprivi as well as Victoria Falls in Zimbabwe (near the point where four countries meet). Shakawe serves the northern-most Panhandle section of the Delta. Other small towns, such as Mahalapye, Palapye and Nata are strung like lonely beads along the A1 and A3 highways that bisect the country.

Population

A total population of around 1.7 million, spread over 580-odd thousand square kilometres, equates to a population density of around only 3 people a square kilometre! And that means overcrowding and traffic jams are not problems you are likely to encounter. A combination of decent education, economic prosperity and a widespread Aids programme promoting the use of barrier contraception has resulted in a population growth rate that is extremely low by African standards. Also unusual in Africa is that the literacy rate for women (80 %) is higher than that for men (75 %). The largest tribal group in the country is the Batswana, who form more than 50 % of the population, followed by the Bakalanga, the Bakhalagari, Herero, Bayei, Hambukushu and Basubiya. These all form part of the Bantu family and are quite distinct from the Khoisan or Bushman tribes who number about 50 000. They are among the last remaining Late Stone Age or hunter-gatherer peoples still living in southern Africa. However, their way of life here has been disrupted by the discovery of large diamond deposits deep in the Kalahari wastelands.

Language

English is the official language and the medium of instruction in secondary schools, while Setswana is the most common language, understood by more than 80 % of the population, and the medium of instruction in primary schools. There are more than 20 other Bantu and Khoisan languages spoken, as well as Afrikaans.

Currency

Botswana's unit of currency is the pula (P) which means rain in Setswana: one

pula is divided into 100 thebe. It is a strong and stable free-floating currency, supported primarily by the country's diamond wealth, tourism and beef production, and there is no monetary black market. Foreign currencies and traveller's cheques are easily exchanged at banks and bureaus de change, and many tourist operators quote prices in US dollars. The exchange rate at the time of going to press was: P6.72 = US$1, P10.25 = £1, P0.91 = ZAR1, P9.18 = €1. Credit cards are widely accepted (including at most lodges) and ATMs are found in all large towns and tourist areas. For up-to-date exchange rates go to: www.xe.com.

Time

Time in Botswana is Universal Time (UT) plus 2 hours – the same as its neighbours (although Namibia does have daylight saving).

Visa requirements

Visitors holding passports from the following countries do not need holiday visas: all European Union countries, the USA, South Africa, Scandinavian countries, and all Commonwealth countries except Ghana, India, Sri Lanka, Nigeria and Pakistan. Holders of other passports should apply to their nearest Botswanan embassy or consulate.

Government

Botswana has a stable and well-functioning multiparty democratic government, based on the Westminster system. Its constitution provides for a republican form of government headed by a president and three main organs of government; the legislature, the executive and the judiciary. A House of Chiefs advises the National Assembly on tribal issues. The dominant political party is, and has been since independence in 1966, the Botswana Democratic Party. The current elected president, Ian Seretse Khama, is the son of Botswana's first head of state, Sir Seretse Khama. All adults over 18 are eligible to vote in elections that are held every five years. The legal system is two-tiered with customary courts (also called *kgotla*) dealing with informal village matters, and the magistrates' courts handling formal law.

Tourist highlights

Botswana is one of the best places in the world to experience what is referred to in these parts as 'the bush' – the African wilderness. Flora, fauna, camping, 4x4 trails, *mokoro* (dug-out canoe) trips, fishing, bird and big-game hunting and any other outdoor activities that you can think of are available in an unhurried, peaceful, non-pushy, clean, uncrowded environment. Phew, quite a mouthful, but it's the truth. National parks like Chobe, and game reserves like Moremi, draw most of the visitors, but there are many other parks and reserves in the country.

The Okavango Delta is a magnet for both game and game-watchers, with *mekoro* (plural of *mokoro*) trips, bird

Being poled sedately through the still, cool and absolutely clear waters of the Okavango Delta in a *mokoro* with a Bayei guide is a highlight of any trip to Botswana.

SOME USEFUL SETSWANA WORDS AND PHRASES

It is customary to start any conversation with a greeting. When addressing a man, *rra*, or a woman, *mma*, use an extended 'r' or 'm', not a double sound. Roll the 'r's and use the gutteral 'g', as in Afrikaans.

Greetings and salutations:

Hello ...	*Dumela rra/mma ...*
How are you?	*O tsogile?*
I am fine	*Ke tsogile*
It's ok	*Go siame*
Go well	*Tsamaya sentle*

Useful words:

Beer	*Bojalwa*
Money	*Madi*
Food	*Dijo* [j as in 'jug']
Meat	*Nama*
Fire	*Molelo*
Water	*Metse*
Lion	*Tau*
Leopard	*Nkwe*
Cheetah	*Letlotse*
Elephant	*Tlou*
Hyena	*Phiri*
Hippo	*Kubu*
Rhino	*Tshukudu*
Buffalo	*Nare*

Zebra	*Pitse*
Crocodile	*Kwena*
Wildebeest	*Kgokong*

Questions and answers:

Who are you?	*O mang?*
I'm ...	*Ke ...*
Yes	*Ee*
No	*Nnyaa*
Do you speak English?	*A o bua Seenglish?*
What is the time?	*Nako ke mang?*
Thank you	*Ke itumetsi*
Which is the road to Maun?	*Tsela ko Maun e kae?*
How much?	*Ke bokae?*
I'm going to ...	*Ke ya ...*

Important signs on toilets:

Men	*Banna*
Women	*Basadi*

watching and fishing as added attractions. The wild game areas of Ngamiland are divided into commercial concessions, which are tendered out on a multi-use basis. Since early colonial times right up to the 1970s 'tourism' in the area equated pretty much to hunting. Since then high-end photographic and adventure travel have supplanted hunting as the main tourism activities. However, the multi-use policy still allows for controlled hunting in many areas.

The lure of learning about the Khoisan culture draws adventurous travellers to the splendid isolation of Tsodilo and Aha Hills. Or if even these out-of-the-way destinations are too tame for you, I'm sure you'll find the solitude you seek in the great salt pans of Makgadikgadi, or the sands of the Central Kalahari. You can rough it, or enjoy some of the most luxurious camps in the world. Read on and all will be revealed.

History and economy 2

Botswana's history and economy have long been linked to its southern African neighbours, over the past two centuries to South Africa in particular. Nomads, farmers, marauding armies, hunters, traders, missionaries, prospectors, politicians – they all had their roles to play in bringing Botswana to its agreeable present.

The old and the new: a traditional mud hut at Shakawe becomes eco-friendly with the incorporation of drink cans into the walls (in the dry air here they won't rust).

History

Peaceful beginnings

There can be few, if any, countries in Africa with a less traumatic history than Botswana. Until the eruption of widescale upheavals during the times of Shaka and other warlords in the early 1800s, there were no serious inter-tribal wars, conflict being mostly settled by expansion into new areas; the mostly benign – and it should be emphasised, mostly unsuccessful – influence of missionaries like Moffat and Livingstone; the benefit of being a protectorate rather than a colony of Britain in more recent times; and a trouble-free transition to independence all contributed to create a stable, peaceful modern state.

But why, one wonders, has Botswana been so successful where many other sub-Saharan African countries have imploded in post-colonial chaos? Maybe because there was apparently nothing there – no-one else wanted the sandy wastelands. The local people were also far greater talkers than fighters and were extraordinarily good negotiators. And when wealth did come their way, in the form of large diamond deposits, they handled it sensibly and without the kind of corruption that dogs many of its neighbours.

It all started tens of thousands of years ago with the San (Bushmen), that perfectly adapted group of hunter-gatherers who left their paintings and engravings on rocks and overhangs all over Africa. The best examples of this art in Botswana can be found in beautiful granitic jumble at Tsodilo Hills. In many ways you could liken the significance that Tsodilo Hills has to the local people, to the importance that Uluru, or Ayres Rock, has on the psyche of Australia's Aboriginal people: both are immense granite outcrops in an otherwise flat place, which seem to draw spiritual energy from above and below.

The San hunter-gatherers were joined, much later, by the Khoi or Hottentot herders, possibly the first people in the world to keep domesticated animals. Genetically there is virtually no difference between the two groups, but what distinguishes them is lifestyle: the San had no stock and no pottery and so are classified as Stone Age; the Khoi had both and so are akin to a Bronze Age culture (perhaps in the southern African context copper would be a more appropriate metallic metaphor).

Farmers, as opposed to hunters, introduced the idea of individual ownership, which in its wake brought the concepts of wealth and leadership. It's even possible that one person could be both hunter and farmer – San and Khoi – in his or her lifetime, depending on their material circumstances. Even the best, most recent archaeology is unable to fully unwrap this prehistorical enigma.

Age of iron

In the first or second centuries AD, Bantu people from Katanga in central Africa arrived with their Iron Age tools and weapons, first arriving via the Chobe and then spreading down the eastern fringe of the country. They were stock and grain farmers and had

A time-old scene: San men dance at their rudimentary grass shelters in the Central Kalahari. But now their continued existence here is a highly controversial issue.

no need to clash with the San and the Khoi – everyone had their own niche. Other Negroid groups related to the Herero and Himba arrived from the west, via Angola and Namibia, while the Bayei river people seem to have followed wetland systems down from today's Congo and Zambia in dug-out boats, much the same as you'll see in the Delta today.

Several centuries later, Bantu-speaking tribes linked to the Shona of Zimbabwe and Venda of northern South Africa built up a trading culture that culminated in an empire that covered much of central southern Africa. Over time the power base shifted geographically, but its greatest expression was Great Zimbabwe (in fact the term 'zimbabwe' refers to the stone building style). Ruined stone settlements of the broader Zimbabwe culture can be seen in the Tuli area around the confluence of the Limpopo and Shashe rivers. It is highly likely that these and other similar ruins gave rise to the fabled 'lost worlds of the Kalahari' as well as kingdoms of gold.

By around 1300 AD the Tswana had become the dominant people of the eastern Kalahari. The founder of the Batswana was, according to oral tradition, the 14th-century chief Mogale. About 150 years later one of his descendents was chief Malope. He, in turn, had three sons: Kwena, Ngwaketse and Ngwato, who became the chiefs of the major tribes that now inhabit Botswana. For a long time this Iron Age culture existed more or less peacefully as cattle farmers, expanding across the Kalahari grasslands as necessary. From around 1800, however, the pressure for good pastoral land in southern Africa reached a climax. The inter-tribal wars we now call the

Originally from central Africa, tribes of the Bantu family make up the majority of Botswana's population.

difecane, or *mfecane*, consumed the subcontinent. This was the time of warlords like Shaka and Mzilikazi. Time and again the Batswana clans were decimated by Mzilikazi's warriors and pushed deeper into the dry lands. They were originally a runaway Zulu group which incorporated all the vanquished people along the way to form a new tribe, the Matabele of western Zimbabwe. Only one Batswana chief, Sekgoma of the Bamangwato clan, was able to withstand the merciless Matabele attacks.

Missionaries and empire builders

After about 30 tumultuous years the conflict exhausted itself and the Tswana prospered again. It was also about this time that heralded the arrival of

the first Europeans who came to hunt and trade. Manufactured goods were brought in and bartered for ivory, leather and ostrich feathers. But all too soon, fuelled by stories of lands of plenty lying empty and waiting, the vanguard of another force of social upheaval turned up: the white Voortrekkers. They were fleeing British rule in the Cape colony and in the late-1830s settled in what were to become the adjoining Transvaal and Free State republics. Conflict between them and the African farmers into whose territories they moved was inevitable.

Missionaries weren't far behind, led by men such as Robert Moffat and David Livingstone of the London Missionary Society. They proceeded to convert – or tried to, with very little real success – the 'natives'. Moffat did, however, translate the Bible into Setswana and baptised members of the Tswana royal family. By the late 1800s the dominant tribe, the Bamangwato, was ruled by Khama the Great, son of Sekgoma. He was something of a visionary who promoted Christian values and foresaw the need for protection during the colonial scramble for Africa. The covetous Germans in South West Africa and the Boers in South Africa held the area in between – what was at the time called Bechuanaland – in a vice.

By 1872 hostilities between the Batswana and the Boers of the neighbouring Transvaal had reached melting point. Khama was the effectual leader of the Batswana people and he appealed to Britain for assistance. In 1885 Bechuanaland was proclaimed a British protectorate (cynics might say the main colonial power of the time saw nothing there worth claiming).

Cecil John Rhodes, the arch-imperialist and millionaire businessman, founder of the De Beers diamond empire, as well as the country he named Rhodesia, then stepped onto the scene. With Rhodesia firmly under his control he turned his attention to Bechuanaland and petitioned the British government to transfer control of the protectorate to his British South Africa Company. The local chiefs, led by Khama, travelled to London (see, talking not fighting) to successfully plead their case and maintain their independence.

However, the Act of Union of South Africa in 1909 provided for the 'eventual' transfer of the protectorate to South Africa. Bechuanaland managed to jog along, with the British trying not to let the protectorate be too much of a financial drain and the chiefs having to regularly argue against incorporation with South Africa. This provision finally fell away in 1961 when South Africa, as a strategy for continuing white political domination, declared itself a republic in 1961 and withdrew from the British Commonwealth.

A country is born

During this time Seretse Khama, son of the late Khama the Great, was being educated at Fort Hare in South Africa and later at Oxford. He met and married an Englishwoman, Ruth Williams, which made him unpopular with the British government, the South Africans, and even many of his own people. However, he returned with his new bride and started to play an active role in politics, forming, with others, the Botswana Democratic Party (BDP) in 1962. As part of the unbundling of the British colonial empire, the country held its first democratic election on 3 March 1965. The BDP won a clear and peaceful victory and Seretse Khama became the country's first prime minister. A year later the constitution was amended and on 30 September 1966, Sir Seretse Khama became the first president of the Republic of Botswana.

Almost as if by the hand of some divine benevolence in return for good behaviour, just a year after independence, large reserves of diamonds were found at Orapa deep in the Kalahari. This allowed the country to embark on a rapid modernisation and upliftment programme which continues today. Hiccups along the way have been caused more by the liberation struggles of its neighbours than internal strife as Rhodesia (Zimbabwe), South West Africa (Namibia) and South Africa – as well as Angola and Mozambique slightly further afield – fought for their own democracies. Botswana managed to stay tacitly neutral and portrayed a steadfast example of stability in the region throughout the tumultuous 1970s and 1980s.

Sir Seretse Khama died in July 1980 and was succeeded by his deputy, Sir Ketumile Masire, who served a relatively trouble-free two terms until retiring in 1998. His deputy, Festus Mogae, became the next president of Botswana and governed quietly and peacefully for 10 years until Sir Seretse Khama's eldest son, Seretse Ian Khama, became

Botswana's fourth president. Ian Khama, former commander of the Botswana Defence Force, has promised four Ds in his presidency: discipline, democracy, development and dignity. In his 1 April 2008 inaugural speech he highlighted alcohol abuse, reckless driving and disrespect for elders as some of the social problems he would tackle and declared himself a democrat who would defend democratic ideals. He promised development in the national infrastructure such as roads, hospitals, electricity and schools and called upon everyone to live their lives and treat others with dignity. Apparently he does not suffer tardiness, so it looks like Botswana is in good hands.

The BDP remains the country's dominant political party but there has always been a strong, mainly urban and younger, opposition to this relatively conservative and somewhat entitled dynasty.

Economy

A country's best friend

The economic history of the country pivots around one crucial date; you could refer to it as BD and AD – before diamonds and after diamonds. That date is April 1967.

As a poor country with few resources or wealth, and very little surface water, Botswana was left alone and in peace by the squabbling superpowers during its pre-independence period. When independence came in 1966, Botswana was ranked one of the world's 20 poorest nations. Then fortune smiled when the Orapa diamond pipe was discovered by De Beers geologist Gavin Lamont and declared to be the second-largest diamond-bearing kimberlite pipe in the world. Two years later he discovered a second huge pipe at Jwaneng, and some time after another one at Letlhakane. Before the recent global recession, Botswana was the world's leading producer of gem-quality diamonds and third biggest overall. Of course, the fact that the wealth has been well used and not squirreled away in politicians' offshore bank accounts is significant.

Other sectors that make a solid contribution to the economy are tourism and beef exports. The government recognises the potential of the tourism industry to grow and create wealth and employment, but follows a policy of low density and low impact. By limiting the numbers of tourists allowed into the game parks and reserves, but charging more, they can generate the same income with less impact on the environment. It's not the most democratic of policies, and highly unpopular with the subcontinent's 4×4-camping fraternity (except in the case of residents who pay a negligible fee for park entry), but it works for conservation.

With cattle forming such an important part of the Botswanan culture, it is estimated that the cattle population is double that of humans. Produced mainly in the Ghanzi area and slaughtered at the Botswana Meat Commission's Lobatse processing plant, most of the meat is exported to the European Community. But the fact that diamonds, until recently, accounted for one-third of the country's GDP and 75% of its exports is of great concern to economists: the diamond sales have dwindled during the present recession, adding to the already pressing problems of high unemployment and HIV/Aids infection rates.

Sobering facts

But to think of Botswana as some fairytale land, as some sources do, would be myopic. Aids aside, there are some economically driven controversies that cannot be ignored, and the first of these is diamonds. A sobering fact is that about half the population still lives below the poverty line. The country does have great wealth but also one of the most unequal distributions of income in the world. International agencies suggest that, per capita, the population is poorer now than it was 10 years ago.

Even more contentious is the case of diamonds versus Bushmen. De Beers, with its partner the Botswana government, retains a large untapped diamond deposit in the Central Kalahari, last stonghold of free-living Bushmen. Since 1985 the government has been moving Bushmen out of the Kalahari in order, it says, to 'modernise' them. But Survival International has spearheaded a protest movement against the Botswana government/De Beers consortium, claiming these are forced removals and therefore the diamonds in question are 'conflict diamonds'. Most significant in all this, perhaps (because there will always be more agendas than we'll know about), is that the Bushmen themselves are resisting the removals.

Cattle versus wildlife

Then we come to the cattle industry. Beef contracts with Europe stipulate that the cattle have to be certified free of any possible contamination by foot-and-mouth disease – which is reasonable enough. But this led to the erection of euphemistically termed

Cattle are not only the pride and joy of most Botswanans, they represent their material wealth. But for travellers they become a real hazard when they stray onto unfenced roads.

'buffalo fences' all around the northern wildlife areas in the 1970s and 1980s. The simple idea was sound enough from a veterinarian point of view, but those fences cut off natural migration corridors – in fact Africa's second largest wildebeest and zebra (and attendant predators and others) migration after the Serengeti. Conservationists raised the alarm; pictures of game carcasses, hanging like wind-dried washing on the game fences, went round the world. Game numbers were decimated, but the authorities – cattle farmers for millennia – were unmoved. The game fences remain and the country's wildlife numbers have shrunk dramatically as a result.

Those darn flies!

Far more effective than the fences for separating wildlife and cattle, though, is the tsetse fly. They carry the parasite that, when bitten by a vector fly, leads to sleeping sickness in humans and nagana in cattle. First it was thought the flies bred in mopane trees (synonymous with southern Africa's major game areas), so a programme to cut down the trees led to widescale deforestation of Ngamiland (Maun was once a densely wooded area). When that proved ineffectual, a programme of spraying ensued. One of the most lethal chemical concoctions ever created, dieldrin, was the preferred poison. Even by the early 1980s when the spraying commenced, it was banned almost throughout the world. Not only is dieldrin apocalyptically toxic, but – like DDT – it does not biodegrade and so accumulates in natural food chains.

What damage this spraying, mainly across the Delta (where there are no cattle, go figure), has caused to the natural ecosystems is hard to measure. But it must be significant.

It is only quite recently the country's decision-makers have accepted that wildlife-based tourism is a viable, long-term economic option ... just so long as it does not affect the cattle. The essential conflict centres around the Okavango, the country's only permanent water source, albeit a fragile one and no more than a film of water on a deep sand basin. Till now it's been the domain of wildlife, but it has always been looked on with great longing by the cattle farmers. As a conclusion, though, the fairest assessment of Botswana is that by comparison not only to its African neighbours, but indeed across the globe, it remains one of the fairest – in all senses – countries in the world.

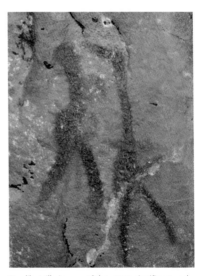

Tsodilo Hills is one of the most significant rock painting sites of the San.

People and culture 3

Tribal differences and definition by ethnic group is not considered politically correct in most of the world today, including in Botswana. But in this chapter I describe some of the roots and origins of customs so as to better understand the past history and present make-up of the country and its people. Historically ethnicity, language and tribes knew no political borders so you'll find many Botswanans share their culture and roots with people of neighbouring countries.

A carefree group of youngsters try their luck at fishing in the Okavango River near Maun.

Culture and customs

The main difference between groupings of people in Botswana is the language they speak. Although English is the official language, the majority of Botswanans speak a Bantu language, while a small minority still cling to their Khoisan roots.

Batswana

Forming about 50 % of the population, this is the main ethnic group in Botswana. Previously from the Magaliesberg region of South Africa, they were forced westwards by Mzilikazi's Matabele army in the 1820s and 1830s. Today they live mainly in the east and there is a still larger number of Tswana people living in South Africa. Because 70 % or more of Botswana's population is able to speak Setswana, the language has become the country's lingua franca and this culture tends to dominate the country.

Bakalanga

The Bakalanga is the second largest group; they live mainly around Francistown, with many more of their cousins across the border in Zimbabwe. They are mainly agriculturalists but also keep cattle and goats.

Bakhalagadi

This is the name given to the various groups who settled in the Kalahari interior. Although customs and dialects differ, their main roots are Sotho (related to the Sotho people in South Africa, mainly in the Free State province) and they keep livestock and cultivate small fields.

Bayei, Basubiya and Hambukushu

These three groups came originally from central Africa and now live in the north of the country, each one around a different stretch of life-sustaining water. The Bayei prefer the Okavango Delta, particularly the shallow southern section where they catch fish from their *mekoro*. The Basubiya hail from the north-west and Chobe region where they cultivate the floodplains. The Hambukushu favour the upper reaches of the Okavango Delta and are agriculturalists, hunters and fishermen.

Herero

This is another group that traces its origins from outside the country and whose numbers are larger in Namibia than in Botswana. Many fled from the Germans of colonial South West Africa in 1904–1905 and settled with their cattle west of the Delta and around Maun. The women of the tribe can be recognised by their long-flowing, bulky dresses and ornate head scarves.

Khoisan

Speaking a host of similar languages, the San (Bushmen) and Khoi (Hottentot) also share physical characteristics such as small stature, light skins, high cheekbones, slanted eyes, tufted hair and thin lips. Traditionally the San have been hunter-gatherers and the Khoi pastoralists and it's amazing that over centuries little has changed. The Kalahari is known as the last home of the San. As competing, largely Bantu, groups moved into areas

Maybe a simple hut on the outside, but every woman's home is her castle.

that were traditionally the domain of the San, they dominated and pushed out these 'little people' who seem to cling to their old customs and find it difficult to adapt.

Everyone admires them for their ancient mystique and old-fashioned ways, but can't seem to find a niche for them in the modern world. Even the Botswanan government, which has been accused of persecuting the San, claim it is only trying to treat them as normal citizens of the country and not as a group of freaks, separate from the rest. NGOs fight for their rights, film-makers document their ways and government agencies try to settle them down in 'nice' controllable villages, but I think the San just want to be left alone. They don't need us, they certainly don't want our interference, and we find that difficult to understand or accept.

Whites, Coloureds and expatriates

How politically incorrect can you get? But it's a reality of Botswanan life that a good number of the people trace their origins back to colonial times. They are people of mixed race who do not belong to Bantu or other tribes but came up from the Cape mainly where the term 'Coloured' was coined (in other places they would be called Creole). While in South Africa apartheid kept them apart and disenfranchised (along with all Bantu 'blacks'), in Botswana no such distinction was made and they are as much citizens of the country as any other.

The white population consists mainly of farmers, originally from South Africa and who still speak largely Afrikaans. Ghanzi is their traditional base in Botswana. But there are also those who come from colonial

In the larger towns styles have become thoroughly modern, while tribal ways persist elsewhere.

formalised religions are represented in smaller numbers, but the majority of Botswanans follow traditional animist beliefs which incorporate great respect for their ancestors and a belief in the spirit world.

Food and drink

If you are staying at a smart hotel or safari lodge, expect a selection of good international cuisine. At the other end of the scale, at roadside eating houses you might find only meat and maize meal (pap). But the one thing you can rely on everywhere in Botswana is good, tasty meat. So, if you are self-catering, stock up with some wonderful steaks, light your fire and get cooking! (Just don't bring it in from outside the country.)

And, while you're slaving over that fire, you are likely to get thirsty so keep an ice-cold beer handy. The local brand is St Louis, a light, very refreshing brew which is available just about everywhere. Botswana also imports all the popular beer brands from its neighbours Namibia and South Africa, which are sold at a slight premium to St Louis. Fortunately the Cape Winelands are not too far down the road, so expect a choice of decent to excellent South African wines – reds, whites, rosés and sparkling (the best being Méthode Cap Classique which is made in true Champagne style). Soft drinks and mixers are available all over the country, as is bottled water, although most tap water is safe to drink. Before buying bottled water, consider that it takes 3 litres of water to make 1 bottled litre, and that most of the plastic bottles end up in landfills or as litter.

administration, trading, artisan and safari backgrounds, and tend to be found mainly in Francistown and Maun. Whatever their origins, they are committed Botswanans and make a good contribution.

The 'expats' are usually skilled or professional people working on contracts who call somewhere else home. But the skills that they bring to the country are much needed and usually shared with and taught to their local colleagues. In fact it is a condition for granting a non-resident a work permit that they train a local understudy into their job.

Religion

Although Botswana is officially a Christian country, only about 20 % of the people are practising Christians. Other

The natural world 4

The natural, unspoilt beauty of Botswana was in danger of being overrun by too many tourists. With a far-sighted, but sometimes unpopular, decision the government hiked the game park fees to a point that brought the numbers back down to a level that the environment can sustain.

A procession of elephants files past Solomon's Wall – a dolerite dyke that would have created a waterfall on the Motloutse River before it was breached – in the Tuli Block.

Past and present

Up to the mid-1970s, Botswana's wild areas were the almost exclusive haunt of big game hunters and a few hardy travellers. It was also when the overland safari business got going, taking small numbers of nature lovers who liked the rough conditions prevalent there. Back then the trip from Francistown to Maun could take a day or more over deep, rutted sandy tracks. In the 1980s, luxury safari lodges catering for game viewing started to replace hunting as the principal wildlife concern in the greater Okavango area, Savuti and Chobe. By the 1990s, safari lodges won, for the first time, formal tenure on their concessions, which meant they could sink more capital into the operations. This led to a general, and in some cases alarming, increase in the degrees of luxury and prices. At the same time, the explosion of the 4×4 industry put great pressure on the country's wild areas. It was decision time.

The natural, unspoilt beauty of Botswana was in danger of being overrun by too many tourists; or, at least, too many of the kind who were not welcome – those who drove their 4×4s around like it was their own playground. With a far-sighted, but sometimes unpopular, decision the government hiked up the game park fees to a point that brought the numbers of visitors to these areas way down. On top of that, the safari lodges catered increasingly for well-heeled overseas clients, rather than regional ones who would spend little on their self-catering camping trips. So, rather than complain about the cost, be thankful that the wilderness is still there for us to enjoy.

For all booking information refer to page 57 in chapter 7.

Some roads in game parks can become deeply flooded: never try to drive through before getting out to test the depth or you could end up as croc food.

National parks and game reserves

Moremi Wildlife Reserve

One wonders what the state of Botswana's wildlife would be today had the hereditary Chief Moremi of the Batswana people not proclaimed Moremi as a game reserve back in 1962. Done in order to preserve the tribe's hunting area, this far-sighted decision showed others that protection was better than exploitation and that rich foreigners would pay big bucks to experience this wilderness.

Enlarged a couple of times since then, it now covers nearly 5000 sq km, including the eastern third of the Okavango Delta. It has since become one of the top wildlife destinations in the whole of Africa. Linked via the Savuti area to Chobe National Park and surrounded by other wildlife management areas, it also allows the migratory game free movement over a vast area.

Most people prefer to visit the reserve in the cooler, drier winter months from April to September when game-viewing, road conditions and comfort levels are generally best. It is also when the water levels in the Delta are at their highest. With water more scarce elsewhere, it becomes a magnate for wildlife and elephant herds up to 300 are not uncommon. However, once the summer rains begin, usually in October, the place comes alive with insect and bird life and generally looks much lusher. It can, however, get very wet underfoot (or wheel), very hot at this time and mosquitoes (and consequently malaria) become prevalent.

You can divide Moremi into two main ecosystems: the drier 'mopane triangle' and the wetlands. The triangle is, needless to say, dominated by mopane trees with occasional sausage trees and various acacias, and open grassland, while riverine forest trees describe the water channels. The wetlands are a mosaic of water channels, low forest-fringed islands and bird-littered backwaters dense with reeds, papyrus and water lilies. The trees of the islands and river banks are jackalberries, ilala palms, African mangosteens, knobthorns and feverberries with waterberry shrubs making up floating islands.

Most types of game are found here – elephant, lion, hyena, wild dog, buffalo, antelope (including sable and roan) and, of course, hippos and crocs. There is even a chance of seeing rhino as they have recently been re-introduced into a specific area. Having a good cross-section of the region's habitats means that a large selection of birds can be spotted in the reserve. The most vocal and spectacular is the African fish eagle, with the silent, rocking bateleur eagle running a close second. Water birds are plentiful and great sightings of herons, darters, egrets and storks are possible. The rare wattled crane and black and slaty egrets are common here, while a sighting of a Pel's fishing owl (they look like big teddy bears in their high tree perches) is, for many people, a highlight of a trip here. Moremi boasts the highest bird count and concentration of any area in southern Africa, with more than half the total of nearly 900 recorded. These include the seldom-seen bat hawk and western banded snake eagle.

The other major drawcard for the mopane triangle area is one of the densest leopard populations in southern Africa and your chances of seeing one here are at least as good as in South Luangwa in Zambia or Sabi Sand adjoining the Kruger Park in South Africa. In the Delta section, specifically Chief's Island, frequently used wild dog dens are almost unique in guaranteeing sightings of this highly endangered predator. Another pack uses the area around North Gate, but not always.

On semi-submerged islands in the Delta, great breeding colonies of storks (including marabous), egrets, herons, ibises, cormorants, darters and other water birds congregate from around September. In the reed beds you are likely to see purple, green-backed and squacco herons, purple gallinules (swamphens), crakes and moorhens. The open water of the lagoons is where white-backed ducks, dainty pygmy geese and jacanas congregate in abundance. As summer approaches, the intra-African and other migrants arrive, including several species of bee-eaters, several cuckoos and raptors including lesser-spotted and steppe eagles, often in large groups.

There are no supplies of fuel, food or drinking water in the reserve, so come well stocked. The tracks are sandy with some deep water channels to cross, and require a 4×4 at all times. Some routes are flooded in the wet season (October to April) and require special skills and a strong nerve. There are rustic, unfenced campsites at South Gate, Third Bridge, Xakanaxa and North Gate, which have been upgraded with showers and toilets.

ABOVE: The Chobe River was once an even bigger watercourse, channeling the Okavango into the Zambezi – until earthquakes sent the Okavango south into the Kalahari basin.

PREVIOUS: The zebra is Botswana's national animal, and the inspiration for the stipes on the flag. Many people will not eat zebra meat though, for fear of inheriting its nomadic ways.

Chobe National Park

This is a big one. At 10 700 sq km Chobe is twice the size of Moremi and is the third-largest reserve in Botswana. The surrounding wildlife management areas and forest reserves increase its size even more, which allows the extensive and free migration of game. First protected as a game reserve in 1961 and then proclaimed as a national park in 1968, Chobe is the most northerly of Botswana's reserves and can be easily visited from Zambia, Zimbabwe (Victoria Falls area) and Namibia's Caprivi Strip.

Like most of Botswana, Chobe is most comfortable in the cooler, drier months, although there is game to be seen all year round. The animals head for the Delta and its various out-reaching channels during the dry months of April to September then disperse into the forests and grasslands in the wet season when there is surface water (pans) there. Giraffe, impala, kudu, plains or Burchell's zebra and blue wildebeest are common throughout the park, along with large predators including lion and spotted hyena. Chobe is perhaps best loved for the big herds of elephants and buffalo which like staying close to the permanent waters of the Chobe and Linyanti rivers. With a large variety of habitats comes more than 450 species of birds, so don't forget your book and binos. Choice sightings would be the African skimmers which breed on sand banks along the river, as well as the cuckoo hawk which reaches the western-most extent of its range here. However, if Chobe has one emblematic species, it has to be the puku, looking a bit like a chubby lechwe, which is found in the rank grasses in substantial numbers at the southern limit of its range.

Except for the far northern section, which is close to the town of Kasane, there is no fuel, food or drinking water available in the park. The tracks are strictly 4×4 and very sandy between Moremi, Savuti and through the Chobe Forest Reserve. During the wet months steer clear of the clayey, black cotton soils of the Mababe Depression and the Savuti Marsh. There are campsites with showers and toilets at Ihaha on the banks of the Chobe River in the north and at Linyanti and Savuti in the south-west. The central Nogatsaa area has no public campsite and is seldom visited by self-drivers.

Kgalagadi Transfrontier Park (Gemsbok National Park and Mabuasehube Game Reserve)

In 1999, the governments of Botswana and South Africa signed an agreement to administer the Mabuasehube Game Reserve and the Gemsbok National Park (Botswana) jointly with the Kalahari Gemsbok Park (SA) thereby creating the world's first cross-border or peace park. Known as the Kgalagadi Transfrontier Park, this is the first of many more such planned cross-border conservation initiatives. Of course the animals have never acknowledged political boundaries, but they've been greatly confounded by human barriers, which these parks seek to redress.

The Botswanan side is covered mainly with sandy duneveld, except for the usually dry bed of the Nossob River which forms the border between the

A cheetah feeds on the plains of the Kgalagadi Transfrontier Park. Springbok are their major prey.

two countries. With the only permanent water coming from boreholes sunk along this river, most of the game is to be seen there. The large camelthorn trees that line the rivers are home to many birds, and in some ways could be considered a distinct ecosystem, or at least habitat, from the surrounding dry lands. Most noticeable are the sociable weavers, which create huge colonial nests that hang in the trees like obscene Christmas baubles; some are so big they break the limbs that support them. A sociable weaver nest can house up to 300 birds, each in its own downy apartment. Each has a false entrance of spiky grass stalks to confuse the boomslangs, cobras and hawks that prey on the sparrow-like birds. On the other hand, these nests offer accommodation to a broad

range of other species including pygmy falcon, pied barbet, chats, red-headed finch and rosy-faced lovebird.

Winter is the most popular time to visit the park, when game is attracted from the dry plains to the watering points along the river. You are guaranteed seeing not only game all day long, but also plenty of interaction and some hectic action too: all things must eat or be eaten out there. However, there are those bird lovers who know the Kalahari in summer is one of the best places in southern Africa to see raptors. There are 82 (at last count) species of raptor in southern Africa and, of those, as many as 30 kinds can be seen in the Kalahari parks. These people brave daytime temperatures in the mid-40s to get their feathers fluffed. Then again, winter visitors have to cope with early mornings around or even below freezing!

Springbok and gemsbok are perhaps the Kalahari specials when it comes to large animals, but the most prized sighting of all is that of the regal black-maned Kalahari lion. The vision of one or more of these potent beasts standing proud against the vermillion-red dunes is a sight never to be forgotten. Also fairly common and frequently seen are cheetahs which, because they hunt exclusively during the day, offer the best chance of seeing a kill.

A feature of the Bots side are the two 4×4 wilderness trails that can be driven in splendid isolation and exclusivity. There are campsites along these trails, as well as in the northern Swartpan and eastern Mabuasehube areas. The Botswanan camps are without amenities; on the South African side the rest camps have hot showers, flush toilets, fuel and shops, but there are also wilderness camps with no amenities there. For the SA side, bookings can be made through the SANParks tel +27-(0)12-428-9111, fax +27-(0)12-426-5500, e-mail reservations@sanparks.org, web www.sanparks.org.

Makgadikgadi and Nxai pans national parks

These two parks adjoin each other and are bisected only by the Nata–Maun main road. Being so easily accessible, they make a good stop-over on the long road to Maun. Nxai Pan is to the north and consists of a series of relatively small, dry pans dotted with picturesque islands. The most spectacular of these is Baines' Baobabs. The famous explorer Thomas Baines passed this way in 1862 and camped under this magnificent group of trees. From a famous painting that he made at the time, it is obvious the trees have hardly changed over the past nearly 150 years.

There is a campsite at Nxai Pan with new ablutions and an informal one near the baobabs. If you do venture there, keep your vehicle well clear of the trees so that their root systems are not compacted and harmed. Also, do not camp under the trees as the effect is the same. Some idiots do, but don't be one of them. There's a good chance of seeing game here which, in the vicinity of these famous, stark trees is most memorable – most often ostriches and gemsbok.

The huge Makgadikgadi Pans are to the south of the main road and offer the adventurous traveller a chance to head out onto a wide expanse of nothingness and experience the stillness and loneliness of total isolation. But be careful: if you get stuck there will be no-one to help you. Be sure to keep to well-established tracks as the pans' surfaces include sink areas from which your vehicle might never emerge once stuck. The western boundary along the Boteti River boasts lush riverine vegetation and is the route of annual wildebeest and zebra migrations.

Try to avoid the pans in the wet season (November to May) as they can become impassable. Even in the dry season you will need a 4×4. This is, however, when huge flocks of ballerina-like greater and lesser flamingos congregate in vast pink swathes. The special place to visit here is Kubu Island, a cluster of granitic mounds protruding from the white salt floor and decorated with ghoulish baobabs. Time a visit to coincide with a full moon and your travel companions will think you a wizard of the occasion.

Makgadikgadi has two public campsites; one at Njuca Hills and the other alongside the Boteti River at Kumaga. The closest fuel is at Gweta (there's also a lodge and basic trading store) but shopping is best done in Maun or Francistown, depending on your route.

Central Kalahari Game Reserve and Khutse Game Reserve

I have left the best for last as the Central Kalahari Game Reserve (CKGR) is the wildest, most challenging and least visited reserve in Botswana. The name says it all: it's in the centre of Botswana, it's in the Kalahari and it's

The gemsbok is the quintessential desert antelope, able to endure extreme temperatures and long periods without drinking.

one heck of a game reserve – a gigantic 52 800 sq km, that's bigger than Holland! Declared a reserve by the British administration in 1961, it was to be a safe haven for the San as much as for the game on which their lifestyle depended. But times have changed: the Botswanan government says it is embarrassed that it should be keeping the San in a reserve, like animals, and wants them out. Others believe it is about the diamonds lying underneath their antediluvian hunting grounds.

The CKGR can be harsh at any time of the year and the game moves around a lot. But don't get obsessed about game; more than just about any other place, the maxim that you cannot guarantee what you'll see applies here.

The attraction is the undiluted wilderness and, anyway, you'll see enough. It's the experience of just being there, the challenge of being self-sufficient in everything that will take your breath away. When the roar of a nearby lion makes your tent vibrate, and you know it's not even trying to be loud, that's when the days of battling through sand seem oh so worthwhile. The sense of cosmic openness will suddenly grip you and give you goose bumps.

Camps and roads are concentrated in the extreme north of the CKGR, and in the Khutse Game Reserve that adjoins the park in the south. For fuel and supplies Ghanzi is closest to the west, Rakops in the north-east and Letlhakeng in the south.

With all the reserves mentioned here, bookings are done through Parks and Reserves Reservations (page 57). Visitors should be totally self-sufficient, with their own camping equipment, food, water and fuel supplies. Camping is allowed only in designated campsites. Each camping area has individually numbered sites, which have a stipulated carrying capacity to avoid overcrowding. Only 4×4 vehicles are allowed in the parks and reserves; the speed limit is 40 kph and off-road driving is not permitted.

It is fatal to sleep outside without the protection of a tent, which should be closed at night. Monkeys, baboons and hyenas are a menace and will steal any food that is not securely locked away in your vehicle. Take all your rubbish out with you or burn it – do not bury it as there are any number of wily beasts that will dig it up. But most of all relax and enjoy yourself.

On the road 5

Not long ago you would not consider visiting Botswana without a tough 4×4
and all the gear to be totally self-sufficient in case of an emergency. This has now
changed and, whether you applaud or decry it, it is possible to do a round trip of
the country without leaving a paved road. New highways and improvements to
existing roads have made it easier to get around. But don't despair; there are still
many rough tracks and difficult-to-find destinations. Let me show you where.

Towing a caravan – even the best off-road 'van – through the sands of Botswana is asking to
get stuck, as this rig did in the Central Kalahari Game Reserve. And then you have to be able to
reverse the thing in tight situations.

Botswana has very good roads and very bad roads, with little in between. The good roads link the country's border posts and main towns, and the bad ones get you to all the interesting places (now that places like Maun, once a real outpost at the end of a bad road, are reached by new black-top).

Main routes and byways

There are basically three main routes in the country, the A1 south to north, the A2 (also known as the Trans-Kalahari Highway) and the A3 from west to east.

Starting in the south at the Ramatlabama border post (which links with Mafikeng in South Africa), Botswana's main highway, the A1, heads north. When it reaches Lobatse, the Trans-Kalahari branches off north-west towards Ghanzi and the Namibian border at Mamuno. Continuing up the A1 you reach the capital, Gaborone, with its fine system of ring roads and freeways. North of Gabs the road is straight and monotonous as it passes through Mahalapye on its way to Francistown, 430 kilometres from the capital. Side roads branch off east to lesser South African border posts and the only important road branching off to the west is to Serowe. The A1 ends a short way north of Francistown, at the Ramokgwebana border post with Zimbabwe and carries on to Bulawayo. But continuing north in Botswana, head out of Francistown to reach the junction town of Nata after 230 km. From Nata keep north for 300 lonely but quite well-wooded kilometres to Kasane in the far north to cross the border there into Zimbabwe, Zambia or Namibia's Caprivi Strip.

The A2 is marvel of tarmac that whisks you from Lobatse, through the deep sands of the Kalahari, bypassing Ghanzi to reach the Namibian border at Mamuno. Going south-east from Lobatse, it crosses the South African border and becomes the N4 to Pretoria. This makes it possible for freight to be transported between Gauteng in SA and the harbour of Walvis Bay in Namibia in double-quick time.

The A3 is another route that used to take days of hard driving through deep sand to get from the junction at Francistown, west across the Makgadikgadi Pans, passing Gweta on the way to Maun at the southern tip of the Okavango Delta. From there it carries on west to Ghanzi. Now it's surfaced and sealed and easy to drive. I suppose we have to blame diamond wealth for the loss of adventure!

But there are still plenty of adventures between these main routes, and most are to be found heading for and in the national parks and reserves. The Kgalagadi Transfrontier Park in the south-west offers the chance to enter from the South African side of the park and do some serious dune riding across to the Mabuasehube section in the south, or Kaa gate in the north and out into even more sand. West of the Delta and close to the Namibian border, you'll find (with the right GPS co-ordinates) Drotsky's Caves, the Aha Hills and Tsodilo Hills.

You could cross the Panhandle section of the Okavango River just north of Shakawe and head down the eastern side of the Delta to two more great 4×4 destinations, Moremi Wildlife Reserve and Chobe National Park. These two parks offer exceptional game viewing and bad roads – just what the 4×4 enthusiast is looking for. The Makgadikgadi, Ntwetwe and Sowa pans between Maun and Nata are not for the faint-hearted as the surface can be treacherous when wet. Finally, there is the huge, isolated Central Kalahari Game Reserve where the toughest are tested and only the San are able to survive permanently.

Road travel

Many visitors to Botswana bring their own 4×4s to experience the off-road adventures that have long been an attraction for visitors. Whether tackling the sands of the Kalahari wastelands or the wetlands of the Delta, you'll need to understand your vehicle and brush up on your driving skills.

Driving on sand

Because a large proportion of Botswana is covered by deep sands, you will encounter many sandy roads. Ideally, you should be driving a 4×4 vehicle,

but no matter what you are driving, deflate your tyres for best traction. Tyre pressures of around 1.2 kPa should do the trick, but as low as 0.8 kPa might be necessary in the most testing situations. Although this makes them more vulnerable to increased wear and tear, it gives the tyre a larger footprint and allows it to 'pancake' instead of digging in when the going gets tough.

The loosest sandy sections should be approached at a slightly higher speed to let your momentum carry you through, instead of trying to power your way through. The real trick here – and it takes some practice to get right – is, when you reach a sustainable momentum to get you through the sand, to run the engine at moderate revs so the tyres don't slip and dig in. It's a fine balance between maintaining sufficient speed and revs. Next, keep the steering wheel and wheels aligned with the track ahead in order to minimise the tyres' frontal resistance. You'll need to select the correct gear before tackling a bad section (usually third, or second

Heavily laden trailers have been the demise of more trans-Kalahari trips than any other cause, leading to stripped gearboxes in some cases.

in worse conditions), because changing gears causes a drop in momentum and that often leads to a full stop. If you do have to change gears, it must be done swiftly and smoothly, while maintaining revs.

Your vehicle should have sufficient ground clearance to negotiate the *middelmannetjie* (central ridge) found on most sandy roads. And stay in the tracks – heading off a well-worn track seldom gives you better traction, and only degrades the environment by creating more scars on the landscape.

Driving at night
Driving after dark should be avoided where possible. Bad visibility, animals on the road and fatigue all contribute to a higher risk. Extra spotlights will help you to see further, but if you must drive at night, slow right down and take great care. Kudus, particularly, tend to try to jump over your vehicle at night on the road, often crashing through your windscreen and causing damage, injury and even death. Cattle could be in the road just about anywhere outside the main parks, and elephants, especially, cross the A1 between Nata and Kasane. Dust on Botswana's gravel roads poses something of a challenge too. Drive with your headlights on, even if they don't help you to see better – with any luck, oncoming traffic will see you.

Negotiating mud and water
If you are not sure of the depth of the mud or water, get out and check and, if it is too deep, reverse out to safety. Move slowly through water so as not to create a bow wave and, if the fanbelt

Congratulations – you've made it to Third Bridge – ground zero for all over-land trips to Moremi.

is in danger of spraying the electronics of your vehicle, remove it. Another danger in deep water is the air intake: you don't want water getting into that (some 4×4s have an air snorkel fitted). And try not to stall with your exhaust under water either — it can get blocked and make starting difficult.

Another potential hazard in Botswana, especially in and around the Delta and on the way to Savuti, is black-cotton mud. Where you see a puddle with blackish mud, it could be just a few centimetres deep, but this soil type has the nasty habit of making 'tank traps' that will grab the strongest 4×4. To get out you'll need the very best recovery equipment and often a second vehicle to assist. Unless you are pretty sure it will 'go', rather get out to check and save hours of sweat and tears.

Driving over rocks and stones

Tyre pressures are important over stony ground – too soft and you will cut the sidewalls, too hard and stones could push right through the tread. There are different opinions on pressures, but I like to ride at pressures recommended for normal highway driving. Just take it easy.

Driving in game parks

Drive slowly and quietly and, most importantly, stay on the road. Never get too close to animals, especially if they are with their young. Many drivers new to game areas (and, sadly, many who are not) ignore animal behaviour, charging up to game and then stopping with a slamming of brakes and a dust cloud. Common sense will tell you what happens next: the game flees. But it's astounding how quickly common sense is thrown out the window by people who want to get closer than the situation dictates. This often applies to tour operators who want to give their clients the best view: all too often neither good sense nor good manners prevail. When you see a potentially good sighting ahead, start slowing down well before you get there, so as not to startle the animal or animals. Then you can gradually move forward, feeling out the situation and letting the game feel comfortable with your presence. You can see when they start to get edgy, and then you should stop, at least for a while before moving forward again. This is how the best sightings and photographs are gained.

Don't get out of the vehicle and never, ever feed any animals. And talking of throwing things out the window, littering is a cardinal sin: carry all refuse with you until you find an appropriate place to dump it. Remember that this is the animal's natural habitat and you are the intruder.

VEHICLE MAINTENANCE

Have your vehicle fully serviced before you go and replace engine oil, spark plugs (petrol engines), air filter, oil filter and fuel filter. Along the way, check the following regularly: engine oil, coolant, transfer case oil, differential oil, gearbox oil, brake and clutch fluid and battery water. Also remove dry grass and seeds from the radiator and chassis.

Without good map-reading skills, a GPS is only a partial tool for navigating back roads.

What to do if you get stuck

To avoid getting stuck in the first place, engage your free-wheel hubs and four-wheel drive long before you need them and keep them engaged even after they are no longer needed. But use your diff-lock sparingly and only if absolutely necessary as it can easily damage tyres, drive shaft and diff. If you do get stuck and haven't broken anything, the first option is to drive out. If you are in mud or sand, try to reverse out of trouble. Stay in the tracks you made going in and, if you manage some movement, rock forward and then back, reversing out a little further each time. A strong push from passengers or bystanders will obviously help a lot. If in soft sand, deflate your tyres as much as you dare (0.8 kPa) and clear a smooth path in front of the tyres in the direction you intend travelling in. If the diff or chassis is resting on the ground, dig it free so that your wheels have weight on them and can grip again.

You will simply dig deeper if you race the engine and spin the wheels. Rather go for option two – being towed out (sometimes it's the first option). If you're driving in convoy, or someone stops to offer help, have a thick, strong towrope or strap ready. If it's long enough, your rescuer won't get stuck too. A rope with a bit of give in it is better than a steel cable.

Option three is 'jack and pack'. A high-lift jack on a wide base is your best bet to get the wheels up and out of trouble. Pack anything – sand, rocks and branches – under all four wheels and lower them back onto solid traction. Sand tracks and mats are useful, but they're bulky to carry, so use what you can find. It's certainly a lot easier to jack a vehicle out of sand or mud than to dig it out. But if you're a first-time user, be extremely cautious of a high-lift jack; one slip and that handle could snap someone's limb. So keep people who are not operating it well clear of the jack. Another trick is to jack the whole back or front of the vehicle free of the ground and simply push it sideways off the high-lift jack, so that the wheels land on firmer ground. A winch (manual or mechanical) is another option but often there is nothing to attach it to. Burying the spare wheel with the winch cable tied to it is hard work, but if you're desperate....

VEHICLE SPARES AND TOOLS

Cut back on this list if you are not straying too far off the beaten track:

- Workshop manual for your vehicle
- Full set of socket, ring and open spanners (compatible with your vehicle)
- Selection of screwdrivers (large and small, Phillips and flat)
- Pliers and a vice grip
- Set of Allen keys (compatible with your vehicle)
- Shifting spanner and monkey wrench
- Hammer
- Spade
- Axe or saw
- Hacksaw
- Set of files
- Wheel spanner
- Two jacks (one high-lift)
- Tyre levers (long and strong)
- Puncture repair kit (including patches, plugs, gaiters and solution)
- Tyre pump or on-board compressor
- Pressure gauge, valves and valve tool
- Two spare tyres and tubes
- Battery jumper cables
- Fanbelts (one universal)
- Engine oil, gearbox oil and brake fluid
- Q20 spray and grease
- Gasket, silicone and contact adhesive
- Tow rope
- Jerry cans (if no on-board auxiliary tank)
- Siphon pump or funnel for water and fuel
- Selection of nuts, bolts, washers and self-tapping screws
- Assortment of rope, string and wire
- Selection of plastic cable ties
- Electric wire, fuses, connectors and light bulbs
- Set of spark plugs and spanner, points and condenser (petrol vehicles only)
- Set each of fuel, air and oil filters
- Spare radiator and fuel hoses with clamps
- Insulation, masking and filament tape
- Pair of warning/hazard triangles (a legal requirement)
- Fire extinguisher (a good one, no toys)
- Spare set of keys (do not keep these inside the vehicle)
- And if you know your vehicle has a particular weakness, make sure you carry the appropriate part.

Breakdowns, punctures and accidents

In case of a breakdown, I have listed breakdown services and repair workshops in as many towns as is practical. If you are planning to venture off-road, then I would recommend you take two spare tyres. In most rugged regions where you are most likely to puncture a tyre, road-side entrepreneurs have set up shop, doing a fine job and providing an essential service. In the unfortunate event of an accident, you will need all the above services – and notify the police (obtain a police report), as well as your insurer, as soon as possible. Emergency numbers for ambulance

A high-lift jack and muscle power will get you out of most kinds of trouble – but that handle is potentially lethal.

and medical assistance are listed on page 62, or under the entry for the nearest town.

Other road tips

Make sure your number plates (especially the front one) are properly secured. The rough conditions that you'll have to contend with can easily tear them off. Cover the front end of your vehicle with a fine net to catch grass seeds and particles (especially during summer). Your radiator could become clogged or, worse still: a build-up of dry grass around your exhaust system could cause a fire and burn out your vehicle. It happens, so check this regularly.

Always plan ahead to have sufficient food, fuel and water – distances are great in Botswana and not every village stocks these basic necessities. Fuel consumption depends on what you are driving and how you are driving, but I have found high-speed highway travel consumes fuel at more or less the same rate as sedate 4×4 travel over flat sandy tracks. Oh, and the wearing of seatbelts in Botswana is compulsory.

As great a country as Botswana is for exploring by motorbike, remember you will not be allowed into game parks and reserves on one. Also, entering the country from the Caprivi through the Mahango Game Park is not possible on a motorbike. Then there is the old problem of sand: driving a motorbike through thick, loose sand can be extremely demanding. If you're not used to this kind of riding, keep your distances manageable or you could end up in the sand pit one time too many, or worse.

Trailers and caravans

Trailers and caravans are fine if you are not going off-road. I have yet to see anything really strong and robust enough to take the beating of seriously rough conditions. If they break down, you have the problem of getting them and your luggage back to civilisation, and even if they don't, they are a schlep to drag around. Sorry, but I'm not in favour of them. Carry what you can in and on your vehicle, and leave the rest behind. The wilderness is not supposed to be too tame. A roof-top or ground tent is sufficient. One word of warning though, in areas where there is large game – and that's most of the country: if you are sleeping on the ground make sure the tent is closed against bugs and predators. There has been at least one case of a camper being taken from his open tent by lions.

What to pack 6

The trick is to take what you need and not burden yourself with items you really won't need. Easier said than done, but Botswana is not Outer Mongolia and there are good shops and suppliers – even where you might not expect them – where you can buy what you need as you go along.

It's in places like the vast expanse of the Makgadikgadi Pans that a map becomes only a partial aid and a GPS indispensible for locating specific landmarks.

Documents

What you can't buy as you go along are your documents and all visitors to Botswana need a passport that is valid for at least six months after entry. You do not need a visa if you are from a country within the European Community, the USA, South Africa, Scandinavian countries or the Commonwealth (except Ghana, India, Sri Lanka, Nigeria and Pakistan). If you do need a visa, it will cost P500 and can take up to 14 days to process. Apply to any one of the following places:

The Botswana Consulate
33 Hoofd Street
Braamfontein
South Africa
Tel +27-(0)11-403-3748

The Botswana Consulate-General
8 Riebeeck Street
Cape Town
South Africa
Tel +27-(0)21-421-1045

The Chief Immigration Officer
Visa Section
PO Box 942
Gaborone
Botswana
Tel 361-1300

Or at one of Botswana's diplomatic missions abroad. They can be found in:

Australia: Botswana High Commission
52 Culgoa Crescent
O'Malley, ACT 2606, Canberra
Tel +612-6290-7500

China: Botswana High Commission
Unit 811 IBM Tower
Pacific Century Place
Beijing
Tel +86-6539-1616

EU: Botswana High Commission
169 Avenue de Tervueren
B-1150 Brussels
Belgium
Tel +32-2-735-2070

Ethiopia: Botswana High Commission
PO Box 22282
Code 1000
Addis Ababa
Tel +251-11-371-5422

Japan: Botswana High Commission
6F Kearny Place Shiba
4-5-10 Shiba Minato-Ku
Tokyo
Tel +81-3-5440-5676

Namibia: Botswana High Commission
101 Nelson Mandela Drive,
Klein Windhoek, Windhoek
Tel +264-61-221-941

Sweden: Botswana High Commission
Tyrgatan 11
PO Box 26024
10041, Stockholm
Tel +46-8-545-25-880

United Nations: Botswana High Commission
80 Rue de Lausanne
1202, Geneva
Switzerland
Tel +41-22-906-1060

United Kingdom: Botswana High Commission
6 Stratford Place
London WIC 1AY
Tel +44-20-7-499-0031

USA: Botswana High Commission
1531–33 New Hampshire, Ave NW
Washington DC
Tel +1-202-244-4990

Zambia: Botswana High Commission
5201 Pandit Nehru Road
Lusaka
Tel +260-1-252-058

Zimbabwe: Botswana High Commission
22 Phillips Ave
Belgravia
Harare
Tel +263-4-794-645

In countries where Botswana has no diplomatic representation, British Embassies and High Commissions can help.

Other documentation

It's always a good idea to travel with a yellow fever certificate (they are valid for 10 years). Although one is not required when travelling from South Africa, you might have been to other countries that will necessitate your having to show one.

When it comes to vehicle documentation, a South African driver in his or her own South African-registered vehicle needs only a valid driver's licence and the vehicle's registration documents. If you are driving a vehicle that is not registered in your name, you will also need

Difficult to reach, Lekhubu Island on Sowa Pan, with its massed granite rocks and baobab trees is a compulsory waypoint.

If you're going your own way, using navigational aids and local knowledge to plan the route ahead should keep you out of trouble.

a letter of authority from the owner on an official letterhead. Visitors from non-neighbouring countries will need a **carnet de passage**. This internationally recognised document (issued by your local automobile association) facilitates customs formalities when crossing borders with a vehicle, and guarantees the payment of duties in the event of the vehicle not leaving the country again (like if it's written off in an accident). The automobile association that has issued it will then have to pay the duties and demand reimbursement from you. If you are a South African and need a carnet for countries further north, or are a foreigner with a South African registered vehicle, contact:

TRAVEL WARDROBE

Here is a suggested clothing list:

- ◆ 2 pairs trousers or skirts – light cotton or synthetic fibre is comfortable and washable, while trousers with zip-off legs double as shorts. Denim jeans are difficult to wash and even more difficult to dry quickly
- ◆ 4 shirts – I prefer collared shirts to T-shirts, they're smarter, cooler and have pockets
- ◆ 2 pairs shorts – it gets hot during the day in Botswana
- ◆ Socks and underwear – they're light and easy to pack, so take at least 4 sets
- ◆ Sweater or hoodie – take a lightweight sweater for summer evenings, but a warm one for winter
- ◆ Jacket – take a light wind- or waterproof jacket for the summer

and a thick, warm one for the cold winter nights
- ◆ Shoes – a pair of light boots or walking shoes, as well as a pair of sandals/slops
- ◆ Cap or sun hat – essential, as the sun can really burn in Bots
- ◆ Towel and swimming costume – you might not want to swim with the crocs in the Delta, but many lodges have pools

Toiletries:

- ◆ Soap and shampoo
- ◆ Toothbrush and toothpaste
- ◆ Hairbrush and nail clippers/file
- ◆ Toilet paper and trowel or garden spade for 'bush patrol'
- ◆ Sanitary towels and/or condoms
- ◆ Shaving kit
- ◆ Towel

Automobile Association (AA) of South Africa, tel +27-(0)11-799-1000, e-mail aasa@aasa.co.za, web www.aasa.co.za.

If coming from South Africa, vehicle insurance that covers you for damage to or loss of your vehicle should be valid in Botswana, but check to be sure. Driver's licences issued in neighbouring countries are valid in Bots, but if you're coming from further afield, bring an international driver's licence issued by your local automobile association.

GPS and navigation

A GPS is not an essential tool for travel in Botswana if you intend sticking to the well-worn routes. However, if you intend being adventurous and tackling some of the wilder areas of the country, I would recommend you use one. Having GPS confirmation that you are at the right spot when you're in the middle of nowhere is very reassuring, although a GPS should never replace your own ability to read a map well and a good sense of direction. I have, therefore, included GPS co-ordinates for those not-so-easy-to-find places. You're probably smarter than me, and able to plot courses and create waypoints with your GPS, but I'm just happy to know that I'm on the right track. As mentioned elsewhere in this guide, my GPS is set to WGS 84 datum (this is important).

- ◆ Sunblock
- ◆ Insect repellent (plenty of)
- ◆ Medicines, including for gyppo guts

Extras:

- ◆ Backpack – a good strong internal-framed one if you are backpacking, or a smaller daypack for short excursions
- ◆ Soft duffel-style bag for internal flights
- ◆ Multi-purpose tool or Swiss army knife: but don't carry this in your hand luggage if you are flying
- ◆ Torch and spare batteries – a head-mounted one is ideal
- ◆ Matches or lighter
- ◆ Notebook and pen
- ◆ Field and travel guides and maps
- ◆ Alarm clock – probably a feature on your cellphone
- ◆ Pocket calculator – also on cellphone

- ◆ Reading material – bird book and some recreational reading
- ◆ Cellphone and recharger – cigarette lighter recharger is perfect (South African and Botswanan networks are compatible but remember to activate international roaming)
- ◆ Plugs and adaptors – to run and recharge electrical gear
- ◆ Universal bath and basin plug
- ◆ Sunglasses and reading glasses
- ◆ Contact lens cleaner and spare spectacles
- ◆ Binoculars
- ◆ Photographic gear
- ◆ Battery recharger for digital and video cameras
- ◆ Washing-up tub
- ◆ Metal bucket (if camping, for making hot water on a fire)

Luxury is one of the most relative concepts of humankind: the camp showers in the Central Kalahari Game Reserve might appear rustic but are pure bliss after a hot, dusty day.

Photography

Botswana is a very photogenic country with wonderful landscapes and skies. You will almost certainly want to photograph the animals and document the happy times you will enjoy. However, unless you are a professional, don't overload yourself with equipment – just lots of film or a big memory card. You are highly unlikely to be able to capture shots better than the professionals, so it is sage advice learned over many trips in Africa that it's far better to take your own 'snap shots' of places and people and buy a good book on the place (there are many on Botswana), than waste time, money and the patience of your travelling companions trying to get the perfect shot every time.

While Botswana has very harsh daylight and is often very hazy (especially in winter when fires are set in the grasslands), it does have beautiful early-morning and late-afternoon

When photographing people, always make sure they are comfortable with you photographing them. Engage them in conversation first, then motion with the camera that you want to take a shot of them and gauge their reaction. Usually, if you have just bought something from them, or they are showing off something of which they are proud, they won't mind.

Although you might be tempted to give sweets or small gifts (pens are always best) to the people you photograph, you will sometimes also be asked for money. Try to resist this, as it encourages a begging mentality: I don't believe holiday photographs should be a traded commodity, but you should give a small token gift or buy a small thing if there is anything for sale from the person or people you want to photograph. A favour for a favour is fair. Maybe you can even help a person with a lift somewhere if it is not too inconvenient. It is too easy to insulate yourself from the realities and the people of the places you visit; this is one way to 'slow down and smell the roses' – call them desert roses.

light, tinged red and orange by the dust particles in the air. Take your photos while the sun is low to capture the colour in your subjects: during the middle of the day, the harsh sun will wash out these colours. Try to take your photographs with the sun behind you and get up close, using a flash for fill-in light on dark subjects. For daytime shots, always use a circular polarising filter, which enhances natural colours and cuts out the glare (but make sure you don't turn the sky blue-black in the process).

For good close-ups of animals and birds, you will need a telephoto lens. Get as close as possible with your vehicle, without leaving the road or disturbing the animals, switch off the engine to avoid camera vibrations and wait patiently for something interesting to happen. If you are hoping to sell your photographs you might still get away with taking slides, but rather make the financial outlay and purchase a digital camera that can shoot in RAW format for quality results.

For the overlander, a night at a safari lodge will feel like absolute decadence, yet some non-African visitors will still feel threatened by a feeling of unguarded openness.

However, this is a massive subject in itself, because then you need a decent computer and processing software and must learn how to use it properly ... it can be expensive and time intensive. As a rule of thumb, to achieve results of a publishable quality, you will need a camera that can capture no less than 5 megapixel images and they will need to be processed as 300 DPI Tiff or Jpeg images (if you don't already know what all this means, just forget it and go the easier route described below).

For your own enjoyment, a simple print-film or digital camera with its own software is fine. So, basically all you need is a camera with zoom lens, memory card or film. Just don't forget the spare batteries as you are unlikely to find the size you need away from large towns. Whatever equipment you do take, make sure it is kept free of dust and out of direct sunlight.

Clothing and personal gear

Botswana is mostly a hot and dry country, but it can get very cold at night during the winter months, so pack accordingly. The country is dusty too, so you will be better off with clothes that don't show the dirt and that wash easily. Morning and evening game drives in winter can be bitterly cold, especially if you go in an open vehicle, so take suitably warm clothes including a beanie and gloves. Modern 'performance' fabrics are easy to wash and dry quickly, requiring no ironing. You'll find them in any decent outdoor store.

A useful tip to make the chore of laundry a little easier (if travelling in your own vehicle) is to seal dirty clothes with water and soap in a bucket with a lid. Stash them aboard a bouncing vehicle all day and they'll be as clean as the proverbial whistle. Thereafter they will only need a good rinse before hanging out to dry.

Eating and sleeping

7

Botswana welcomes everyone and offers food and accommodation no matter what your budget or preferences are. Visitors can choose from bush camping to luxury lodges, self-catering to banquet buffets all at prices that offer good value for money.

It's amazing what luxury can be created in a tented camp, like this bathroom at Haina Lodge in the Central Kalahari. The modern safari lodge is perhaps the most sublime blend of modern comforts and wilderness.

Accommodation

Visitors to Botswana generally come for an outdoor experience. They want to wear shorts and sandals while viewing game from a safari vehicle or *mokoro* and the country has built up an expert industry offering those activities. Comfortable accommodation is offered in the game parks and on the waterways, as well as convenient overnight facilities along the way. Many of the private game lodges in the Delta and surrounding areas offer board and lodging that far exceed the simple description of 'comfortable': while merely comfortable might have been what you got 20 years ago, today the trend is to offer fantastical safari accommodation in the wild bush.

One of the reasons why the standard of accommodation is so high in Botswana is that the tourism board regularly inspects and grades all accommodation establishments (although some operators complain it forces them into a formal structure they do not necessarily want, which forces prices up). Facilities are categorised as guest houses, hotels, game lodges or camps. Accommodation lists are available from the Botswana Tourism Board, tel 391-3111, web www.botswanatourism.co.bw.

Botswana can offer some of the most luxurious game lodges in the world, but you pay. Rates for the top places are quoted only in foreign currencies and can spike to around US$2 000 a night a person in high season! Other lodges are available at more reasonable prices, but will still cost at least P1 000. Top hotels

Roughing it is a relative term and camping is what you make of it. What it does do is bring you close to the feeling of the wilds.

CAMPING CHECKLIST

The following is adequate, but feel free to add to my Spartan choice:
◆ Tent with built-in ground sheet and mosquito net (vehicle roof-top tents are easy and safe)
◆ Camp stretcher and/or foam mattress
◆ Sleeping bag and inner sheet
◆ Pillow
◆ Light folding camp chairs and table
◆ Lamp (first choice should be a fluorescent type that works off the vehicle's battery)
◆ Clothes line and pegs
◆ Wash basin and soap

in Gaborone will charge you about P1 000 a night, but guest houses and hotels in other towns range from around P150 to P300 a person a night. The biggest bargains, however, are found in camping, as often a top lodge or hotel will have an adjoining campsite where the rates are seldom more than P80 a person. Other campsites can cost as little as P30 a night and there are a few backpackers – Gabs and Maun – where dorm rooms are available at P100. Rates quoted in this book (2010) should be the final price paid and include hotel levies and VAT. But that does not stop you from trying to negotiate lower rates, especially out of season when places are not full.

Park bookings

Booking and payment for entrance to and camping in the national parks and game reserves of Botswana has never been easy, and it's just got a whole lot more complicated. At the time of going to press the situation was the following: Entrance fees to all national parks and game reserves for citizens of SADC countries (including South Africa) was P120 per person per day plus P50 per vehicle per day, except for the Kgalagadi Transfrontier Park and Mabuasehube where the fees are P20 per person and P20 per vehicle. Fees must be paid in advance (except sometimes you can talk the ranger at the gate into accepting a late payment) to the

GRUB'S UP!

You may want to consider some of the following cooking ingredients, but remember that all the items listed here can be bought in Botswana:

Durables

- Selection of canned meat, fish and vegetables (just a few for emergencies – they're heavy!)
- Selection of dehydrated foodstuffs (also only for emergencies – some are disgusting)
- Breakfast cereal or muesli mix
- Powdered milk
- Tea and/or coffee
- Powdered isotonic drink
- Crisp bread or crackers
- Biscuits or rusks
- Salt, pepper, herbs and spices
- Stock cubes and garlic
- Dried fruit and nuts
- Rice and pasta
- Cooking and salad oil
- Honey and/or jam
- Peanut butter and/or Bovril
- Bottled water, cold drinks and beer

Semi-durables

- Bread
- Potatoes, onions, cabbage and carrots
- Apples and oranges
- Cheese and margarine
- Bacon and salami

Perishables

- Meat
- Eggs
- Salad
- Tomatoes
- Soft fruit

Perfection – a loaf or bread, salads, *krummelpap* and you, in the wilderness. All that's missing here is the beer – or wine if you are more classically inclined.

Department of Wildlife and National Parks. Their head office is in Gaborone at tel 318-0774 or 397-1405, fax 391-2354 or 318-0775, e-mail dwnp@gov.bw or dwnp.parrogabs@gov.bw, web www.gov.bw. They also have branches in Maun (tel 686-1265, fax 686-1264), Francistown, Kasane, Ghanzi and Kang. The above department also accepts bookings and payments for the campsites at South Gate and Xakanaxa in Moremi Wildlife Reserve and Ihaha in Chobe National Park. Many of the public campsites that were previously run by the DWNP have now been privatised. Bookings and payments for

ON THE MENU –
THE PERFECT *KRUMMELPAP*

Krummelpap, or one variation of the local staple pap, is a stiff, crumbly porridge made with mealie (maize) meal. Not to be confused with smoother *stywepap* or wetter, porridge-like *slap-pap*, it is best enjoyed with braaied boerewors and gravy and cooks well over a fire in a black, cast-iron pot.

The ratio of water and mealie meal is crucial and must be one to one: one cup of water and one cup of meal makes one large helping.

Pour the water into the pot, with a generous pinch of salt and a dessert spoon of butter for each cup of water. Bring to boil, add meal, place lid on pot, do not stir or turn down heat. Leave for a few minutes and then stir. Leave on low heat with lid on for 20 to 30 minutes, stirring occasionally. The consistency must be dry and crumbly (if not, add more meal). It sounds simple, but a good *krummelpap* takes time to perfect – so good luck.

campsites at Kwai at Moremi's north gate, and Savuti and Linyanti in Chobe National Park are handled by Mapula Lodge, tel 686-5365/6, fax 686-5367, e-mail sklcamps@botsnet.bw or conniem.mapulalodge@info.bw. Rates for SADC citizens are P200 per person per night (plus park fees payable to the DWNP). The campsites at Third Bridge in Moremi and Nxai South and Baines' Baobabs in Nxai Pan National Park are the responsibility of the Xomae Group, tel 686-2221, fax 686-2262, e-mail xomaesites@botsnet.bw and they charge P150 a day plus P50 for a trailer. Sunday Pans, Piper and Kori campsites in the Central Kalahari Game Reserve have been entrusted to Big Foot Tours, tel 395-3360, e-mail bigfoot@gbs.co.bw who also charge P150. Other camps in Khutse and the CKGR are still handled by the DWNP. The campsites in Mabuasehube and the Kalagadi Transfrontier Park are still the domain of DWNP at the reasonable rate of P30 per person per day. Good luck!

Each town and region mentioned in this book has a list of accommodation and eating options, most of which will suit the budget of the average visitor to Botswana. I have not listed the very luxurious lodges, which are usually booked as part of a package holiday and not really within the scope of the self-drive tourist.

Camping tips

Choose your site well – avoid game tracks or dry river beds that might flood, and try to find shade under a tree. In game areas, use your wits a

OUTDOOR COOKING CHECKLIST
◆ Cooker and fuel
◆ Icebox or small fridge (the compressor type is best)
◆ Barbecue grid in a bag, pot stand
◆ Sack of wood or charcoal
◆ Firelighters and matches
◆ Pot (a traditional black, cast-iron pot is ideal for over a fire)
◆ Frying pan and kettle
◆ Plates and bowls
◆ Chopping board and sharp knife
◆ Mugs and/or glasses
◆ Cutlery and can opener
◆ Washing-up bowl, soap and cloth
◆ Paper towels and refuse bags

bit, and avoid camping too close to water where animals might try to gain either access or exit. The results could be uncomfortable for you and the animals (remember, hippos come out the water at night to feed, so be especially careful to give them a wide berth because they can be extremely dangerous).

A flat site with soft ground or grass and some bushes to protect you from any prevailing wind is ideal. Your tent should be as comfortable as you can carry – it will be your home for the duration of your trip – and should also be easy to erect. If you are sleeping in a roof-top tent, then an awning off the side of your vehicle will provide protection from the sun and cool of the evening. Whether you sleep on a mattress on a groundsheet or

COUNTING THE COST

Here are some average prices charged at supermarkets in the larger towns:

◆ Loaf white bread	P5	◆ Boerewors (1 kg)	P37
◆ Mineral water (1 l)	P6	◆ Beef mince (1 kg)	P40
◆ Can of beer	P7	◆ Eggs (1 doz)	P13
◆ Can of Coke	P4.25	◆ Bully beef (300 g)	P10
◆ Milk (1 l)	P10.75	◆ Cooking oil (750 ml)	P13
◆ Washing powder (1 kg)	P20	◆ Tea (100 bags)	P19
◆ Lettuce	P8	◆ Instant coffee (250 g)	P19
◆ Potatoes (1 kg)	P6	◆ Sugar (1 kg)	P7
◆ Onions (1 kg)	P6	◆ Rice (1 kg)	P14
◆ Frozen chicken (1 kg)	P24	◆ Rump steak (1 kg)	P50

carry stretchers depends on you, and the use of a sleeping bag depends on the time of year: a warm down-filled sleeping bag for winter and merely a cotton liner for the hot summer months.

I like cooking as much as possible on a fire when in the bush, but try not to burn too much scarce wood with a huge bonfire. For a quick cuppa when there is no fire, a simple gas cylinder and ring should be enough. Camping can become very complicated with too many gadgets and equipment and my advice is, always, KISS (keep it simple, stupid). On the other hand, some campers are gadget freaks who can't resist a new thing; and then there is the question of persuading your partner along – which could include portable showers, toilets, hair dryer connections.... It's your trip.

Importing animal products into Botswana

Based on an agreement with South Africa, you are allowed to bring the following animal products into Botswana:

- ◆ Red meat   25 kg a family
- ◆ Poultry   5 kg a person
- ◆ Eggs   36 a person
- ◆ Milk   2 litres a person

This is when crossing from SA only and not from any other neighbouring country. But, in practice, it depends on any outbreak of animal diseases in Botswana or its neighbours. You might then run into roadblocks and have your animal products confiscated – vacuum packed, frozen or fresh is all treated the same. I've heard of holiday families sitting at the roadside braaiing and gorging themselves on their pre-packed meat rather than have it confiscated. As the situation changes with time, contact the Dept of Agriculture, tel 495-0753, e-mail nbok@gov.bw or gbathuse@gov.bw. The best strategy for a somewhat confusing and potentially expensive problem is to buy all your meat in Botswana – it's very good. But even then you may not be allowed to carry it from one district to the next.

Health and safety

8

Botswana's hot, dry climate is generally healthy and there is a good network of state-run hospitals and clinics. The population is small, there is little overcrowding, few slums and a there is a good amount of wealth to spread around. There is also very little serious crime (light fingers notwithstanding), so relax and enjoy your visit.

It might look like paradise, but the 'serpents' here are tiny mosquitoes that are most active around dusk and dawn. You need to protect yourself against their bites and the possiblility of malaria.

Travelling out of your own environment and comfort zone always exposes you to new germs, a change of drinking water with its own microbes and new sets of safety situations, so it is best to take some precautions before you travel to Botswana.

Start by consulting your doctor or a travel clinic for advice and the latest information on the health situation in the country. Have a dental check-up and organise a supply of any special medicines you require. Spectacles can break and contact lenses are easily lost while travelling, so think of taking spares. If you are really going into the wilds, you might even consider taking an emergency do-it-yourself (or with the help of a friend) dental kit.

I have listed the state-run hospitals and clinics in the towns where they occur, as well as private doctors and hospitals. If you are in need of any medical assistance and are staying at a hotel or lodge, speak to the staff, they are best able to organise medical help.

Medical insurance

Make sure your medical insurance will cover you if you need an air-lifted evacuation back home. Your existing medical aid might cover this, and some credit cards do as well if you have used them to book a flight, but read the fine print and make sure you're sufficiently covered. If not, contact one of the following companies, which specialise in this sort of insurance cover:

Travel Guard
Tel +27-(0)860-110-848
e-mail travel@dnanet.co.za
web www.travelguardinsurance.co.za

Europ Assistance, Johannesburg
Tel +27 (0)11-991-8000
e-mail info@europassistance.co.za
web www.europassistance.co.za

Netcare 911, Johannesburg
Tel +27-(0)860-638-2273
e-mail customer.care@netcare.co.za
web www.netcare911.co.za

Immunisation

Although Botswana does not normally require yellow fever vaccination certificates, you will be asked for one if you have come from an infected area (especially countries to the north). If you travel a lot, have it done – it's valid for 10 years. You might also consider a precautionary anti-tetanus shot and, while you're at your doctor's, discuss cholera, hepatitis, typhoid, tuberculosis, polio, meningitis and rabies. It's a scary list and you probably won't come across any of them, but it's best to be informed.

Along the way

I have listed doctors, dentists, clinics, pharmacies and hospitals in the towns I cover in this guide. If there is a serious emergency that requires evacuation, don't hesitate to phone the number

---

EMERGENCY NUMBERS
- Ambulance   997
- Fire Brigade   998
- Police   999

Commercial rescue services
- Rescue One   392-3249
- Netcare   991
- Medrescue   911

that your medical travel insurance policy quotes – make sure you have the number and policy details handy at all times.

Tap water in municipal areas is treated and safe to drink, but bottled water is also available. Just consider the negative environmental hazards of buying bottled water for the perceived convenience. Hygiene standards are good and it is safe to eat at restaurants and takeaways, but if you do pick up a stomach bug then rest up, stop eating and drink lots of fluids. If you dehydrate as a result of diarrhoea or too much sun, you might need a rehydration fluid. Bought in sachets and mixed with water, they consist mainly of the salts and sugars that your body needs. They can also be replicated with a flat Coke and salt, or Bovril, sugar and water.

For your personal safety beware of the animals, and I don't just mean the

wild ones. Yes, wild animals can be dangerous and should be treated with caution, but the stray domestic ones can also be deadly. More people die on the roads of Botswana after hitting stray cattle, donkeys or goats than from attacks by wild animals. Don't speed, drive alert and if you have a choice, avoid travelling at night.

Malaria

Although not as virulent a threat as in some other, more tropical, parts

Donkeys that stray onto the roads are some of the most dangerous animals in Botswana.

STATE HOSPITALS AND CLINICS

Bobonong Hospital
261-9223

Francistown Jubilee Clinic
241-1544

Francistown Nyangabgwe Hospital
241-1000

Gaborone Princess Marina Hospital
595-3221

Ghanzi Hospital
659-6333

Gumare Hospital
687-4002

Gweta Hospital
621-2333

Goodhope Hospital
548-6236

Hukuntsi Hospital
651-0030

Jwaneng Hospital
588-0271

Kanye Hospital
544-0333

Kasane Hospital
625-0333

Lentsweletau Clinic
577-9205

Lerala Clinic
495-4019

Letlhakane Hospital
297-8242

Lobatse Athlone Hospital
533-0333

Mahalapye Hospital
471-0333

Maun Hospital
686-0444

Mmadinare Hospital
261-7236

Mochudi Deborah Hospital
577-7333

Molepolole Livingstone Hospital
592-0333

Moshupa Clinic
544-9225

Orapa Hospital
297-2557

Otse Clinic
533-7655

Palapye Hospital
492-0333

Pitsane Clinic
548-6289

Rakops Hospital
297-5111

Ramotswa Lutheran Hospital
539-0212

Sefhare Hospital
494-8201

Sefhophe Clinic
261-8214

Selebi-Phikwe Hospital
261-0333

Serowe Memorial Hospital
463-0333

Thamaga Hospital
599-9250

Tsabong Hospital
654-0232

Tutume Hospital
298-7249

STATE DENTAL CLINICS

Francistown Oral Health
241-3480

Gaborone Oral Health
391-3991

Kasane Dental Clinic
625-0333

Maun Dental Clinic
686-0448

Selebi-Phikwe Oral Health
261-1434

Serowe Oral Health
463-0533

of the world, malaria is prevalent in Botswana. This common infectious disease is spread by female mosquitoes when they first bite an infected person and then pass the disease on to a healthy one. They transfer tiny parasites that multiply in huge numbers, causing fever, other life-threatening symptoms and sometimes death in the case of cerebral malaria. The symptoms start as if for flu, but quickly get worse until they erupt in a head-splitting, body-shaking fever.

Mosquitoes breed wherever there is water or even damp ground, so the risks are higher in the wet season or around the Delta. It is possible to build up a slight immunity to the disease, but even people living where malaria is common can still contract it. Babies and young children are most at risk, which is why so many deaths occur annually in this age group. Pregnant women are also particularly at risk. The disease can be spread only through human vectors, so it will be most common in places where people live (which can include safari lodges).

Your first line of defence against this disease is to avoid being bitten by mosquitoes. They are most active at dusk and dawn, so keep them at bay with appropriate clothing, covered doors and windows and sleep under a mozzie net. If you must go outdoors, cover yourself and use an insect repellent. The use of preventative drugs while travelling in an infected area can help, but is not necessarily a guarantee against infection. With various prophylactic drugs there are some warning symptoms that you should not ignore: chills, headache, muscular pains, vom-

BASIC FIRST-AID KIT
- First-aid manual
- Malaria prophylactic tablets
- Aspirin or paracetamol (for fever, pain or to gargle for a sore throat)
- Antiseptic cream for disinfecting cuts and abrasions
- Adhesive bandages (both strips and rolls)
- Gauze bandages and cotton wool
- Antihistamine for allergies and to ease the itch from bites and stings
- Thermometer (standard body temperature is 37°C)
- Insect repellent
- Analgesic eye drops
- Analgesic ear drops
- Scissors and tweezers
- Safety pins
- Water purification tablets (a few drops of iodine also works)
- Sealed and sterile syringes and needles
- Sunblock and burn gel
- Throat lozenges
- Flu remedy

Optional extras:
- Malaria cure
- Antibiotics
- Vitamin tablets
- Diarrhoea cure
- Rehydration mixture

iting, diarrhoea and particularly fever. Some medications should not be taken by pregnant women, those using oral contraception or anyone using other medication. Consult your doctor or pharmacist about medication.

After visiting a malarial area, if you

feel the symptoms of flu – fever, shivering, headache and perspiring – it's a fairly sure sign that you have contracted malaria. Get to a local doctor, clinic or hospital immediately. Because it is such a common disease in places like Botswana, local medics should recognise it and know how to treat it. Showing any of the above signs when at home in a non-malarial area is even more dangerous when no-one recognises them. This can happen anything from a week to a year from being in an infected area. If it does happen, tell your doctor where you have been and ask him to run a malaria test. There are drugs that easily cure malaria and you should suffer no after effects from the disease or the treatment – but you'll need to catch it early.

As malaria has built up immunity against many older drugs, the pharmaceutics profession is continually developing new ones. Consult your doctor or a specialised travel clinic for the latest info on the disease, how to prevent it, and how to treat it.

Some travel clinics in South Africa

Medi-Travel International operates travel clinics in the following centres:

Pietermaritzburg +27-(0)33-342-9348
Cape Town +27-(0)21-419-1888
Pretoria +27-(0)12-348-5245
Sandton +27-(0)11-706-7710
or look them up at www.meditravel.co.za

Netcare Travel Clinics is a network that caters to the medical needs of travellers at:

Pretoria +27-(0)12-421-6805
Cape Town +27-(0)21-419-3172
Durban +27-(0)31-582-5300
Port Elizabeth +27-(0)41-365-2070
web www.travelclinic.co.za

The Travel Doctor Africa also has clinics in most major centres. Call +27-(0)11-214-9030 to locate your nearest one.

To keep up to date on malaria via some interesting websites, try:

www.who.int/ith/countries/en
www.who.int/topics/malaria/en
www.malaria.org
www.cdc.gov/malaria
www.malaria-reference.co.uk

You need to ensure your net is well closed, as a mozzie will sometimes spend all night trying to find a way in.

Getting there and around 9

Botswana welcomes tourists and has a good road and transport system. The adventurous would say 'too good!'

An exciting flight in a light aircraft is sometimes the only way to reach a camp in the Okavango Delta – though afternoon flights will be very bumpy.

Getting there by road

From South Africa

At last count there were 17 border posts between South Africa and Botswana, from Kgalagadi Transfrontier Park in the south-west, to the Tuli Block in the east. Most of these are dusty little outposts down lonely dirt roads and used mainly by local shoppers and traders.

Border posts on main touring routes are: Ramatlabama, which links SA via Mafikeng with the southern end of the A1 highway in the south-east corner of Botswana; Pioneer Gate/Skilpadshek which links Pretoria, via Zeerust, to Lobatse in Botswana and the choice of the A1 north to Gaborone and beyond or the Trans-Kalahari Highway past Ghanzi and on into Namibia; and Martin's Drift/Groblersbrug, which links South Africa's N11 from the north of that country to Botswana's A1 at Palapye. All of the above borders are accessible by normal vehicles.

From Zimbabwe

There are only three routes between Zimbabwe and Botswana and none is very busy. The main border crossing is at Ramokgwebana/Plumtree, which links Bulawayo in Zim to the northern end of the A1 highway and Francistown. Further north is the tiny Pandamatenga border crossing, which would get you into Botswana from Hwange, and lastly the Kazungula border post (not the ferry) gives you access to Chobe and Kasane from the Zimbabwean tourist town of Victoria Falls.

From Zambia

With the border between Botswana and Zambia a mere GPS position at the confluence of the Chobe and Zambezi rivers, the only crossing point is via the Kazungula Ferry. This bustling, exciting spot is pure 'old Africa' with long waits under the huge trees that line the banks. It is popular with tourists from nearby Livingstone and trans-Africa truckers.

From Namibia

There are two borders that give access to Botswana from the Caprivi. In the east is Ngoma Bridge across the Chobe River, forming a link between Katima Mulilo in Nam and Kasane in Bots. The other is in central Caprivi at Mohembo, close to Shakawe and the Panhandle of the Okavango River. Both these border

---

CROSSING INTO BOTSWANA

Border crossings are swift and painless compared to some African countries, but you will need:

◆ A valid passport which must be valid for at least 6 months after the date of return from Botswana
◆ Visa (not for South African passport holders – see page 15, 48 for a list and exemptions)
◆ A nationality sticker for your car (ZA for South Africa)
◆ Registration papers for your vehicle
◆ Money to pay cross-border vehicle charges – P50 for a Short Term Permit, P20 for the Road Safety Levy and P50 for 3rd party insurance

posts offer great options for combining your tour of Botswana with a long loop through Namibia.

The other two crossings with Namibia are along Botswana's lonely western boundary. Mamuno is by far the most popular of these as it is on the Trans-Kalahari Highway which starts in Walvis Bay, passes through Windhoek and Gobabis in Namibia, runs down to Lobatse in Botswana and exits again into South Africa to end in Pretoria. The other is the little-known and little-used Dobe border post between Tsumkwe in Namibia's Bushmanland and the Aha and Gcwihaba Hills area of Botswana. This isolated, sandy route is only for the well-equipped traveller looking for adventure and a special stamp in his passport.

A final, slightly convoluted, but interesting crossing is through the Kgalagadi Transfrontier Park. This route allows passage between Botswana, South Africa and Namibia by simply passing through the game reserve. Border officials are posted in the park and the route can offer a handy shortcut or holiday alternative.

Getting there by bus

Intercape, which is based in Cape Town, runs luxury buses to Botswana, Namibia and Mozambique. Its only route into Bots is a daily run from Joburg to Gaborone and back. It leaves from Johannesburg's railway station at 14h30 and arrives at the Kudu Shell petrol station in Queen's Road, Gabs at 21h10. It returns at 06h30 the next morning, arriving in Johannesburg at 13h00. The cost is ZAR220 for a single ticket. For further information tel 397-4294, or in South Africa +27-(0)21-380-4400, e-mail info@intercape.co.za or web www.intercape.co.za.

AT&T Monnakgotla is a Botswana-based travel and tour company that operates a luxury coach service between Gaborone and Windhoek, via Kang, the Mamuno border post and Gobabis in Namibia. It runs in both directions every Friday and Sunday, leaving the main bus station in Gabs at 07h00 to reach the Thuringerhof Hotel in Windhoek at 18h00. In the opposite direction, a bus leaves Windhoek at 06h00 and reaches Gaborone at 17h00. The fare is P390 or N$440. Contact them on tel 393-8788, e-mail at-t@monnakgotla.co.bw, web www.monnakgotla.co.bw.

Getting there by air

The only international flights into Botswana are from the neighbouring countries of South Africa (from Johannesburg or Cape Town), Zimbabwe (Victoria Falls) or Zambia (Livingstone). This means that if travelling from further afield, you would have to fly via one of these places.

Air Botswana, although expensive, has the best service and flies four times a day between Gaborone and Johannesburg, daily from Jo'burg to Maun and three times a week to Harare in Zimbabwe. Contact them in Gaborone on tel 395-1921, e-mail info@airbotswana.co.bw or web www.airbotswana.co.bw. In Johannesburg tel +27-(0)11-975-3614, or in Harare on +263-4-793-228. In Cape Town tel +27-(0)21-671-5802.

Air Namibia flies four times a week

between Windhoek and Maun and on to Vic Falls. They can be contacted on tel +264-61-299-6333, e-mail customercare@airnamibia.com.na or web www.airnamibia.com.na.

Getting around by road

Botswana has roads of all types. The wide, new surface of the Trans-Kalahari Highway welcomes international traffic from Namibia and South Africa. A wide network of good, tarred roads from Gaborone to Kasane and onwards to Maun and Shakawe keeps the wheels of commerce rolling around the country. Dirt roads and tracks that criss-cross the wilder areas entice tourists who are looking for that special off-road experience.

Local drivers are mostly courteous and adhere to the rules of the road – even the taxi drivers! The traffic police do their duty without harassing you, but do set regular speed traps, so stick to the speed limits. Animals that stray onto the road, both wild and domestic, are a real danger so keep your speed down and keep your eyes peeled, especially if travelling at night. Some tarred roads are badly potholed, in spite of the fact that the government has sufficient funds to repair them.

Getting around on public transport

In addition to the international bus

CROSSING BORDERS

The following are just a few personal suggestions on the protocol to follow when crossing any border.
Patience and politeness are the keys, always:

◆ Approach the border slowly and sedately; make no commotion or disturbance.
◆ Park sensibly, in the correct area, without blocking others.
◆ Dress properly – at least sandals, shorts and shirt – and take off any cap, hat or sunglasses.
◆ Wait your turn – unless it's a complete free-for-all.
◆ Greet and smile at all officials, act politely and never make snide, whispered comments.
◆ Laugh only if it is good natured and can be shared.

◆ Expect polite treatment, but don't make an international incident out of official rudeness – it is only you who will suffer.
◆ Have all your documents ready.
◆ Make sure you have been to both customs and immigration and have obtained all the stamps and documentation.
◆ Don't smuggle anything – you could be searched and will have to bear the consequences.
◆ Avoid all bribery – ignore or act dumb to any hints of it and never suggest it.
◆ Offering a cold drink to a sweating official in a hot border shack, however, will oil the wheels.
◆ Once the formalities have been completed, don't rush off and do be prepared to stop if asked.

Air Botswana keeps the main safari areas connected with domestic and international flights.

connection between Gaborone and Johannesburg (page 69), there are regular intercity buses that ply the main routes around the country. But with no dominant national coach companies, bus services are a local affair with no networks or published timetables. Each large town has a bus station where you'll find transport to the next large town, as well as minibuses that service the nearby villages. The small towns are serviced by the intercity buses as well as having their own minibus services.

All rail passenger services in Botswana have been discontinued.

Getting around by air

Because distances in Botswana are so great and overland travel into the arid areas and the waterlogged Delta is difficult, flying is a popular way of getting around. Air Botswana has a domestic network that flies out of the hub at Gaborone to places such as Maun, Kasane and Francistown (see page 69). There is also a busy fleet of charter aircraft with Maun as the centre of activity. Game-viewing flights are offered and most lodges have their own land-

ing strips for guests to fly in to.

Some of the popular charter companies based in Maun are:

Sefofane, tel 686-0778, e-mail sefofane@info.bw

Delta Air, tel 686-0044, e-mail synergy@info.bw

Mack Air, tel 686-0675, e-mail mack.air@info.bw

Northern Air, tel 686-0385, e-mail nair@kerdowney.bw

Guided tours

As with any country that's a popular tourist destination, Botswana offers a wide selection of options and prices. Levels of luxury also range from budget backpackers to celebrity luxury. Take your pick:

Wilderness Safaris offers tailor-made or fixed itineraries in top-of-the-range luxury. Contact them in Johannesburg on tel +27-(0)11-807-1800, e-mail enquiry@wilderness.co.za, web www.wilderness-safaris.co.za.

Wild Frontiers offers a similar service, but also offers budget options. Their details are tel +27-(0)11-702-2035, e-mail reservations@wildfrontiers.com, web www.wildfrontiers.com.

Others include **Crocodile Camp** based in Maun (www.crocodilecamp.com), **Desert and Delta** (www.desertdelta.com), **Gunn's Camp** in the Delta (www.gunns-camp.com), and **Okavango Tours and Safaris** (www.okavango.com).

For horseback safaris the two options are:

Macatoo (www.africanhorseback.com) and **Okavango Horse Safaris** (www.okavangohorse.com).

For Central Kalahari trips, the best options are **Penduka** (www.pendukasafaris.co.za) and **Deception Valley Lodge** (www.dvl.co.za).

If you are keen to visit Botswana in your own vehicle, but want to go in a group, then maybe a guided self-drive safari is for you. Try **Explore Africa Adventures**, tel +27-(0)21-663-5319, e-mail info@explore-africa.co.za or web www.explore-africa.co.za. Or contact **Taggallongg** at tel +27-(0)11-975-3293, e-mail tagalong@global.co.za, web www.taggallongg.co.za.

The grand circle tour

Finally, what about planning your own grand round-southern Africa trip? Presuming you started in the south at Cape Town, you could head up north to the Namibian border at Noordoewer, wander up the coast via the Fish River Canyon, Lüderitz, Sossusvlei and Swakopmund and from there head inland for the Etosha Pan. From there you would swing east through the Caprivi Strip to enter Botswana through the Mahango Game Reserve to Shakawe, head south down the Panhandle, dropping in at Tsodilo Hills and Drotsky's Caves to Ghanzi.

Then drive across Botswana, through the Central Kalahari Game Reserve to the Makgadikgadi Pans and up to Maun. After a visit to the Okavango Delta, there would be Moremi, Savuti and Chobe to see before crossing the Kazungula Ferry into Zambia. A visit to the famous Victoria Falls, and then east through Lusaka to South Luangwa National Park before entering Malawi. There you would have to visit Monkey Bay and Cape Maclear on Lake Malawi (or further north up the lake if you're looking for more adventure), before heading south through Blantyre and Milange into Mozambique.

From Quelimane on the coast, your route should take you across the Zambezi at Caia and through the Gorongosa National Park to Beira. Stuffed with prawns and Dois M beer, your next destination would be down the coast at Vilankulo before heading inland across through the newly opened transfrontier park to Pafuri in the north of the Kruger National Park. From there you could take your pick of routes back down to Cape Town (the Drakensberg, Great and Little Karoos seem to beckon) to complete the trip of a lifetime!

Practical
information 10

Listed alphabetically, the information in this chapter should answer all your questions and smooth the way through this fascinating country.

This selection of authentic San handicrafts is proudly on offer at Gantsi Crafts, Ghanzi.

Airport departure tax

There is no airport departure tax for either domestic or foreign flights in Botswana. However, some operators of flights into the Delta from Maun will levy a surcharge.

Angling

Angling is not permitted in the national parks and game reserves, which leaves the Panhandle south of Shakawe and the Chobe River around Kasane as the best areas. Drotsky's Cabins and Shakawe Lodge around Shakawe, the Swamp Stop at Sepupa, and Guma Lagoon Camp near Etsha 13 are good places to drop a line in the Panhandle. Around Kasane most lodges will rent you a boat and supply tackle, but the keenest fishermen seem to be at Ngina Safaris. See appropriate regions for info on these places.

Fish to go for include tiger, nembwe, African pike, barbel and several species of tilapia (bream). While the tiger is the fish most anglers covet, Bots has yielded some world-record tilapia. In the Panhandle and main Delta, the most amazing fishing phenomenon is the annual catfish run. Every year, sometime between August and November, shoals of hundreds and sometimes thousands of catfish 'run' through the shallow papyrus reed banks hunting smaller fish. They slap their tails on the surface of the water to stun their prey, creating a frenzy of activity that attracts other predators such as crocodiles, snakes, fish eagles, herons and storks – a unique spectacle.

To halt the spread of the devilish, almost uncontrollable 'Kariba' weed (it's actually from South America), the import of boats from other countries is strongly discouraged. Any foreign boat or canoe must have a temporary import permit which is issued by The Secretary, Water Apportionment Board, Private Bag 0029, Gaborone, tel 360-7100.

Birding

Botswana is a magnificent birding destination with a range of natural habitats from very dry to very wet, each with its own variety of resident and migrant bird species. The Okavango Delta is southern Africa's and indeed one of the world's great birding hot spots, offering water of varying depths as well as extensive reed beds, backwater lagoons, riverine forests and drier island areas. The Palaearctic and intra-African migrants arrive from the north during September and October and remain until April or May, while the local rains (October to April) create new life in the form of fruits, berries and insects for birds that are nesting and breeding. Pans that flood during this time are always a magnet for aquatic birds, while the savanna area thorn trees offer nesting opportunities for others.

On top of most birders' specials lists will be Pel's fishing owl, slaty and black egret, carmine bee-eater, night and green-backed heron, wattled crane, African skimmer, four species of roller, several kingfishers, too many rare passerines to mention and of course a long list of raptors. Rather than trying to list them all here, I recommend that you visit the following excellent web sites:
www.birdlifebotswana.org.bw
www.birdingbotswana.com

A good field guide, binocs, camera and sun hat — and you're set for hours of rewarding birding anywhere in the country, even hotels that have lush gardens.

www.sabirding.co.za
www.africanbirdclub.org

Car hire

There are three international car hire companies operating in Botswana:

Avis, Gaborone Airport, tel 391-3093, e-mail botswanares@avis.co.za, web www.avis.co.za.

Budget, Gaborone Airport, tel 390-2030, e-mail botswana@budget.co.za, web www.budget.co.za.

Europcar, Gaborone Airport, tel 390-2280, e-mail info@europcar.co.za, web www.europcar.co.za.

There are also some South African companies that will hire out 4x4 vehicles for cross-border travel:

Britz, tel +27-(0)11-396-1860,

e-mail info@britz.co.za, web www.britz.co.za.

Bushlore Africa, tel +27-(0)11-792-5300, e-mail info@bushlore.com, web www.bushlore.com.

KEA, tel +27-(0)11-230-5200, e-mail info@keacampers.co.za, web www.keacampers.co.za.

And one in Botswana:

Self Drive Adventures, Maun, tel 686-3755, e-mail selfdrive@ngami.net, web www.selfdriveadventures.com.

Communications

Telephone

The Botswana Telecommunications Corporation (BTC) operates the country's reliable fixed-line telephone service. Not only is it quick and easy

ON CALL!

The country code for Botswana is 267. There are no area codes to dial and each telephone number has seven digits. You can recognise the origin of the number by the first digit or digits.

- 24 Francistown
- 29 Letlhakane
- 26 Selebi-Phikwe
- 3 Gaborone
- 46 Serowe
- 49 Palapye
- 53 Lobatse
- 54 Kanye
- 57 Mochudi
- 58 Jwaneng
- 59 Molopolole
- 62 Kasane
- 65 Ghanzi
- 68 Maun

Dial 192 for national directory enquiries or go to: www.btcdirectory.co.bw.

to phone within Botswana, but international calls in and out of the country are equally good. BTC also has public phones spread around the country in cities, towns and villages. These operate with coins or phone cards, which are on sale at post offices, garages and shops.

Mobile phones

There are three mobile phone operators, BTC, Mascom and Orange. Coverage is good and includes all towns and cities and main routes that link them. Coverage does not (thankfully) extend into wilderness areas. International roaming agreements are in place, so your home-based mobile phone should work here. All operators sell Sim cards for around P30, as well as pre-paid vouchers.

Internet

Post offices in the larger towns offer an internet service and there are internet cafés around the country.

Courier services

EMS offers an express mail service through the post office, which means more than 40 service points in the country, as well as international links. Contact them on tel 390-0963, web www.botspost.co.bw.

DHL offers its world-famous service from 12 branches around the country. Contact them on tel 391-2000, web www.dhl.co.bw.

Botswana Couriers also has an extensive network with branches in the five largest towns. Tel 393-0629, web www.botscouriers.co.bw.

Credit cards

Visa and Mastercard credit and debit cards are accepted in Botswana and the number of ATMs is growing all the time.

Customs regulations

You can bring personal, sporting and recreational goods into the country and your duty-free allowance is:

- Wine 2l
- Spirits 1l
- Cigarettes 200

You can also bring in the following foodstuffs (subject to health controls):

◆ Red meat   25 kg a family
◆ Poultry   5 kg a person
◆ Milk   2 l a person
◆ Eggs   36 a person

Vehicles, caravans and trailers from neighbouring countries may enter on a temporary import permit, but vehicles from further afield will need a carnet (see page 50). Boats and canoes may not be imported without a difficult-to-obtain permit from the Department of Water Affairs (see page 74). Firearms need a special police permit issued by the Central Arms Registry, PO Box 334, Gaborone. As Botswana's currency is strong, there is no cross-border restriction on banknotes, but any amount over P10 000 must be declared.

Electricity

Botswana's power is rated at 220 volts with wall plugs of both the round three-pin variety (South African), or square three-pin (UK). The thinner two-pin type that is in use for recharging mobile phones is also quite common; hotel bathrooms usually have a shaving point that will take this kind of plug.

Embassies

American Embassy, Government Enclave, Gaborone, tel 395-3982

Angolan Embassy, Private Bag BR111, Gaborone, tel 390-0204

British Council, The Mall, Gaborone, tel 395-3602

French Embassy, PO Box 1424, Gaborone, tel 397-1733

German Embassy, PO Box 315, Gaborone, tel 395-3038

Namibian High Commission, PO Box 987, Gaborone, tel 390-2181

Netherlands Consulate, PO Box 457, Gaborone, tel 390-2194

South African High Commission, Private Bag 00402, Gaborone, tel 390-4800

Zambian High Commission, PO Box 362, Gaborone, tel 395-1951

Zimbabwean High Commission, Government Enclave, Gaborone, tel 391-4495

Hunting

Botswanans make money out of their animals, tame and wild. Like game viewing and photographic safaris, hunting is just another way to do so. Played within the law and the rules of a fair chase, it is supposed to be done in a sustainable, ethical way and the local people benefit from the proceeds.

Inhabitants of a region have control over the game on their lands by way of a government concession, which can be utilised for hunting or game viewing – or both in different sectors and seasons. The game is regarded as a valuable resource that is generally worth more to a foreign tourist than in the food pot of a distant kraal. So the animals are protected by the very people who would probably be killing them in other countries. If you are against the idea of hunting you need not worry about coming into contact with this in Botswana. Hunting is discreet and never mixed with non-hunting activities.

However, there are always the exceptions. Citizens are allowed to hunt on their own lands whenever they want to, for a small licence fee. Also, some hunting operations are not as ethical as others. Particularly worrying is the diminishing numbers of lions as hunters go for trophy males. When none is available, and a hunting client has paid a lot for the licence and the trip, the shooting of sub-adult males has been known. Biologists were so worried about a possible collapse of the country's lion populations, that on 24 October 2007 the Wildlife Department suspended lion hunting indefinitely.

Floating down one of the most pristine stretches of water in the world with a beer and rod in hand — the living is easy and who cares if the fish are biting or not!

IVORY ISSUES

The Convention on International Trade in Endangered Species (Cites) gave Botswana the go-ahead to sell 43.6 tons of ivory at the end of 2008. Cites established the authenticity of the ivory source after checking the paper trail, data base and the physical ivory. The lifting of the ban on the sale of this ivory was welcomed locally (of course not by all) as it would provide income from controlled hunting, while still protecting the species as a whole.

Even more contentious for some is that, after years of total protection following lobbying by international wildlife conservation bodies, elephant hunting is currently permitted in Botswana. The other side of this coin is that, because of its outstanding conservation record, elephant numbers in some areas exceed the carrying capacity and the habitat is in danger of damage if numbers are not controlled (the Chobe River and central Savuti areas particularly). Whatever your sentiments, bear in mind that it was hunting that led to the preservation of these wild areas in the first place, and it has its role to play in ecotourism and conservation.

We cannot recommend any hunting outfitter, but if you want to, google 'hunting safaris botswana' and you will find several links. For the record though, Safari South is the oldest hunting operation in the country (www.safarisouth.org).

Gaborone and the south-east

11

I know most of the readers of this guidebook will not spend much, if any, time in Gaborone, but it is the capital of the country and one of the fastest-growing cities in southern Africa and so deserves a good look-around.

Gaborone is one of the most healthy, pleasant and low-rise of cities you'll ever visit. It's like the perfect capital of a near-perfect land – and it's for real.

The amazing thing about Gabs, as it's generally referred to, is that it hardly existed 40 years ago. Until Botswana's independence in 1966 it was the village of Chief Gaborone of the Batlokwa people, while the country was administered from Mafikeng in South Africa. Building of the town started in the mid-1960s and was initially slow until diamond wealth accelerated growth in the 1980s. Although it is still small by international standards (fewer than 250 000 inhabitants), it now has all the ringroads, glass high-rises and sprawling shopping malls of its bigger brothers around the world.

The official Botswana Department of Tourism brochure for Gabs has six shopping malls on the list of top seven places of interest in the city. The other one is Kgale Hills, a panoramic view site. This is the unfortunate truth about Gaborone: there is very little of interest for the tourist to see and do here. But let's see what we can find to keep you busy while you're here.

The focus of capital is the Main Mall, which is less of a shopping area and more like the Pall Mall of London (well, maybe just a little). It is a double-laned thoroughfare in the centre of the city, with Parliament House and its gardens at the western end. The mall itself houses shops, banks, hotels, offices, post office and at the eastern end is the National Museum.

The National Museum illustrates the culture and history of the country through collections of artefacts and interesting dioramas. Outside are larger exhibits – an old steam engine and a coach. The complex also houses the National Art Gallery, where one can appreciate the works of local artists, and a curio shop, where indigenous crafts are on sale. There are other places of interest surrounding Gaborone, which I have listed at the end of this chapter.

Getting there

By road

If you are entering Botswana from the south, you'll probably use the Ramatlabama gate from Mafikeng, or Pioneer Gate from Zeerust. In both cases you'll pass through Lobatse. The Shell garage in the centre of this southerly town sells fuel (obviously), takeaways and has an ATM. Look out for the quaint St Mark's Anglican Church in the main street. This stone-walled and thatch-roofed church was built in 1934 and is now a national monument. Lobatse is dominated by the Botswana Meat Commission (BMC), reputedly Africa's largest abattoir. With most of the commercial cattle ranched in the Ghanzi District to the northwest, it is well situated to process all of Botswana's beef exports, the majority of which go to the European Community.

Just north of the BMC in this long, spread-out town you will come across a smart shopping mall, which contains a Barclays Bank, OK supermarket, chemist, dental clinic and Engen petrol station.

Next up is the large and multiroomed Cumberland Hotel, which offers spacious, en-suite standard double rooms with TV, air-con and coffee making facilities for P485, budget singles for P295, and family rooms (sleep 4) for

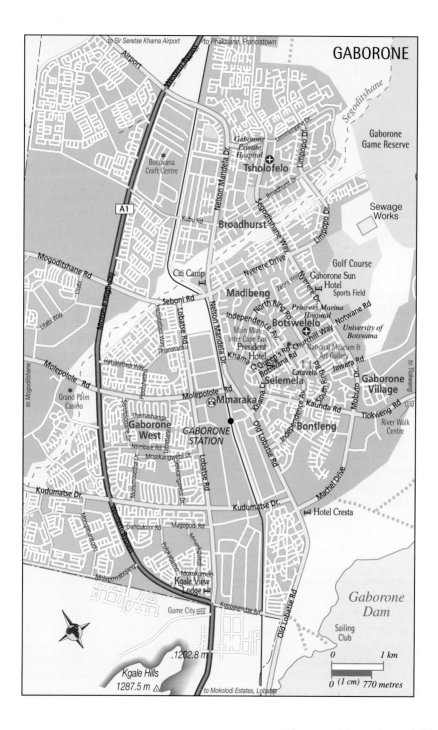

GABORONE

to Sir Seretse Khama Airport   to Phakalane, Francistown

Airport

Western Bypass

Gaborone Game Reserve

Segoditshane

Botswana Craft Centre

Nelson Mandela Dr.

Gaborone Private Hospital

Lemmenyane Dr.

Tsholofelo

Limpopo Dr.

Broadhurst Dr.

A1

Kubu Rd

Broadhurst

Segoditshane Way

Limpopo Dr.

Sewage Works

Mogoditshane Rd

Litabi

Golf Course

Citi Camp

Nyerere Drive

Gaborone Sun Hotel

Zebra Way

Sports Field

Seboni Rd

Madibeng

North Ring Rd

Nyerere Dr.

Notwane Rd

Litabi Way

Mandela Highway

Nelson Mandela Dr.

Lobatse Rd

Hatslatladi Way

Independence Av.

Princess Marina Hospital

Botswelelo

University of Botswana

Molepolole Rd

Hatsalatladi Way

Thanasanku

Main Mall, Inter Cape Bus, President Hotel

Khama Cr

Queen's Rd

Churchill Way

National Museum & Art Gallery

to Mogoditshane

Pelotshetha

Botswana Rd

Caravela

Jawara Rd

to Tlokweng

Grand Palm Casino

Molepolole Rd

Mmaraka

Selemela

South Ring Rd

Gaborone Village

Themashanga

Serobolamo Dr

Gaborone West

GABORONE STATION

Kaunda Rd

Mobuto Dr.

Ntimbale Rd

Mosekangwetsi Dr.

Lobatse Rd

Independence Av.

Bontleng

Tlokweng Rd

River Walk Centre

Kudumatse Dr.

Kudumatse Dr.

Old Lobatse Rd

Machel Drive

Hotel Cresta

Gandukumi Rd

Magogodi Rd

Mmankgodi

Polokwathebe

Molapowabojang

Mokukumelo

Kgale View Lodge

Game City

Kgobaseretse Rd

Old Lobatse Rd

Gaborone Dam

Sailing Club

0   1 km

0 (1 cm) 770 metres

.1202.8 m

Kgale Hills
1287.5 m △

to Mokolodi Estates, Lobatse

P550. No meals are included in these rates, but there is a restaurant, pool and large attractive gardens. Tel 533-0281, e-mail cumberland@botsnet.bw. There is a large hospital just past the hotel, and the grand, new High Court of Justice is on the outskirts as you leave Lobatse.

Continuing towards the capital, look out for a left turn-off 10 km south of Gaborone to Mokolodi Estates. This is where you'll find the Mokolodi Nature Reserve and Mokolodi Backpackers, two accommodation establishments described later in this chapter. The first traffic circle as you enter Gaborone is flanked by the large Game City shopping mall on the left and an industrial area on the right. Turn left at the circle to join the Western Bypass, which takes you around the city and north to Francistown, or keep straight to reach the city centre. A right turn at this circle would bring you to the Old Lobatse Road and access to the eastern part of the city.

If approaching Gaborone from the east, you would have entered Botswana from South Africa via the Tlokweng border post. Tlokweng Road brings you in past the River Walk Shopping Mall and bisects Machel Drive, which acts as an eastern bypass. Continue straight across it if you want to reach the centre of the city.

Coming down from the north, the main A1 highway reaches Gaborone at a traffic circle and the intersection with Nelson Mandela Drive. Turn left if you want to head through the centre of Gabs along Nelson Mandela, right takes you to the airport and straight ahead keeps you on the Western Bypass, avoiding most of the traffic and returning you to the A1 to Lobatse at the traffic circle at Game City.

By air

Botswana's only international air links are to Harare and Johannesburg, but both Air Botswana and South African Airways operate daily 1-hour flights to Joburg for all international connections. Air Botswana also flies internally to Maun, Kasane and Francistown. The Sir Seretse Khama International Airport is out past the Walmont Ambassador/Grand Palm Casino complex along Airport Road.

By bus and train

Intercape operates a daily service to Johannesburg from the Kudu Shell service station in Queen's Road in the Main Mall. It departs there at 06h30 and reaches Joburg Station at 13h00. It leaves Johannesburg again at 14h30, to arrive back in Gabs at 21h10. Tickets cost P200 one way, and there is a small Intercape office behind the garage. Local buses and taxis radiate out in all directions from the chaotic and sprawling bus station next to the train station in Molepolole Road in the centre of the city.

The largest intercity bus company in Gaborone is AT&T Monnakgotla. It runs daily return services with fast luxury coaches from Gabs to Palapye (6 hours), Tsabong (6½ hrs) and Hukuntsi (6 hrs). The buses also run between Hukuntsi and Jwaneng (4½ hrs) and between Serowe and Molopolole (4 hrs). It also operates an international service every Friday and Sunday between Gaborone and Windhoek and back. Coaches leave Gabs' central bus station at 07h00 and arrive at the Thuringerhof Hotel in Windhoek at 18h00, while another coach leaves Windhoek at 06h00 to arrive in Gabs at 17h00. A single trip costs P390 or N$440. Tel 393-8788, e-mail at-t@monnakgotla.co.bw, web www.monnakgotla.co.bw.

All rail passenger services in Botswana have been discontinued.

Getting around in Gaborone

Gaborone has four arterial roads, all running in a south–north direction. The Western Bypass (Motsete Highway) serves mainly as a through road and boasts a few shopping malls and fuel stations alongside it. Lobatse Road is a continuation of the highway up from Lobatse and ends at the city centre bus station. Nelson Mandela Drive is a continuation of the Old Lobatse Road

(if coming from the south, turn right at the Game City traffic circle) and runs right through the centre of the city to rejoin the A1 to Francistown. And Machel Drive turns to the right off the Old Lobatse Road and serves as an eastern bypass of the city. Access to the Tlokweng border post is off Machel Drive. All roads are well sign-posted and the traffic is never too jammed up.

Staying in Gaborone

The city offers all levels of accommodation, from camping to five-star luxury. It is also your best overnight stop in this south-eastern region if you are heading north. All accommodation listed has safe parking unless otherwise stated.

The most elegant hotel in Gabs is the Walmont Ambassador Hotel, formally the Grand Palm (S24° 38.471, E25° 52.785). Situated on the Molepolole

As is the case of the whole country, the population of Gaborone is small, but youthful and growing. But only moderately so, with one of the lowest growth rates in Africa.

Road just off the Western Bypass, it is set in a large manicured estate which also houses a casino and convention centre. Its plush interior boasts smart pubs and cocktail bars, intimate coffee shops, the Beef Baron Steakhouse and Livingstone Buffet. There is also a health club, hairdresser, business centre and ATM in this top-class establishment. Rooms are luxurious and quite reasonably priced at P1100 (double or single). For even more luxury, try a suite at P1700, or the over-the-top presidential suite at P4145 (in case there are any presidents reading this guidebook). Tel 363-7777, e-mail info@gp.walmont.com, web www.walmont.com.

The Gaborone Sun is more centrally positioned on the eastern bypass road (where Machel Drive morphs into Mobuto and then Chuma Drive) and also has all the trappings of a top hotel. There are restaurants, pubs, casino and business centre, but it lacks the class of the Walmont. Rates are P1805 single and P1925 double, but presidents stay in their suites at P6265 and P6385 if they bring the first lady (or other). Breakfast is included for all. Tel 361-6000, e-mail natsales@sunint.co.za, web www.suninternational.com.

The 'African chic' Mondior Hotel is a superbly finished, high-tech hotel aimed at the discerning business traveller. Located close to the Tlokweng traffic circle on Mobuto Drive, the Mondior offers studio, 1-bedroom or 2-bedroom luxury suites. Each unit has a lounge area with a dining table and kitchenette containing a refrigerator, microwave, kettle and toaster. Another feature is the trendy News Café pub and restaurant adjacent to the hotel. Studio rooms are P800 a night (sleep 2) 1-bedroomed suites P1000 and 2-bedroomed suites P1500 (sleep 4). Tel 319-0600, e-mail info@gab.mondior.com, web www.mondior.com.

The rather tired-looking Cresta Lodge is easily accessible on Machel Drive and is set in large grounds with a pool and children's playground. It offers the usual business centre, coffee shop, restaurant and bar, but is not good value at P1005 single and P1140 double. Tel 397-5375, e-mail reslodge@cresta.co.bw, web www.crestahosp.co.za.

The Metcourt Inn is a smart, neat, business-like, value-for-money hotel on the same estate as the Walmont Ambassador (so you can share casino and other amenities). More of an upmarket motel than a hotel, it is excellent value – in hotel terms – at P520 (single or double) for a standard room and P600 for an executive room. Tel 363-7777, e-mail metres@grandpalm.bw, web www.metcourt.com.

For longer stays in the centre of the city, Motheo Properties offers serviced, self-contained apartments at plot 4710, Moremi Road, off Independence Avenue. All units have a fully fitted kitchen with washing machine as well as an air-con and DStv. Daily rates are P398 for a double studio and P655 for a 2-bedroomed apartment. Longer term rates are available on request. Tel 318-1587, e-mail motheo@info.bw, web www.motheoapartments.co.bw.

The Kgale View Lodge is a smaller B&B establishment, set in the residential area just across the road from Game City as you enter Gabs from the south (cross the circle, take the first left

While there is no shortage of comfortable to luxury hotel accommodation in the capital, there are also camping options for self-sufficient and budget travellers.

and first left again). Rates, inclusive of breakfast, are P440 single and P450 double (hardly worth differentiating). But they are often full, so book ahead on tel 312-1755.

Getting into the budget category, you'll find Brackendene Lodge on Tati Road, off Independence Avenue, near the Main Mall. There are spacious en-suite rooms with air-con, TV and coffee-making facilities and a simple dining room, which offers inexpensive meals. Rates are P370 single and P410 double, inclusive of breakfast. Tel 391-2886, e-mail brackendene@mega.bw, web www.brackendenelodge.com.

If you are arriving by bus and need to duck into the safety of a hotel as quickly as possible, the Gaborone Hotel is con-veniently situated between the bus and train stations. Not bad, considering the dodgy area, they charge P336 double including breakfast – but I wouldn't leave my vehicle unattended there! Tel 392-2777, e-mail gabhot@info.bw.

The only centrally situated camping facilities are at Citi Camp at the intersection of Nyerere and Nelson Mandela drives. Difficult to find (S24° 38.062, E25° 54.595), it looks as though it might close down soon, and the security looks suspect. Currently though, nice shady sites with adequate ablutions are available at P75 a person a night, and they also have double rooms (sharing ablutions with campers) at P390. Tel 7244-6067.

A much better bet if you want to camp

ABOVE: Visit the craft market in Gabs for traditional handicrafts, mostly basketware.
PREVIOUS: Gabs by night — most of the action is cosmic.

is to head for the Mokolodi Estate on the Lobatse Road, 10 km south of the city (turn-off S24° 44.703, E25° 49.833). There are two establishments there – Mokolodi Backpackers, and Mokolodi Nature Reserve. Closest to the main road is Mokolodi Backpackers, a pleasant, safe, home-from-home operated by the friendly and helpful Hendrik Wierenga, who will look after you as his personal guest. He offers camping at P75 pp, dorm accommodation at P135 and neat, tastefully furnished double chalets at P285 – all very good value.

Land line is 7411-1165 or mobile 7161-0036, e-mail info@backpackers.co.bw, web www.backpackers.co.bw.

The Mokolodi Nature Reserve is at the end of the estate road and offers more of a bush experience with game drives, traditional dancing and nature walks on their 10 000-acre reserve. The restaurant dishes up sumptuous bush braais, while accommodation is available in self-catering chalets overlooking a waterhole (3-sleeper week night rate is P420) or campsites (P80 an adult a day). Tel 316-1955, e-mail information@mokolodi.com, web www.mokolodi.com.

There is one last place you can try for camping, the St Clair Lion Park. This establishment runs a kiddies fun-fair and has a few lions in small camps. Situated further out past Mokolodi on the road to Lobatse, they also offer picnic and campsites at P70 for a day visit and P110 to overnight.

Eating, drinking and entertainment in Gaborone

Although not known as the fun capital of the world, Gabs has a few hot spots where you can get down and enjoy yourself. Most of the shopping malls dotted around the city have decent restaurants. River Walk Mall, out on the Tlokweng Road, is the most promising of the lot and has the always popular and trendy Primi Piatti Restaurant as well as a Spur Steak Ranch, Nando's Chicken and Debonairs Pizza. It also has cinemas showing current movies, and the Abyssinia Coffee House for great coffee and Ethiopian specialities on Friday nights. Game City Mall at the southern entrance to Gaborone has an O'Hagans Irish Pub (popular for sundowners), and more cinemas.

If you tire of all these clones of South African franchises, seek out Caravela Portuguese Restaurant in Mokgosi Road, off Independence. A bit more pricey than the chains, they produce wonderful, tasty steaks and Portuguese specialities and have a decent wine list. They are popular for business lunches and evening dinners, so book first at tel 391-4284. All the big hotels have pubs and restaurants, the best being the News Café at the Mondior Summit Hotel and the selection of eateries at the Walmont.

If you fancy feeding your money into a noisy flashing-light machine, or throwing it away on a table, there are many casinos in Gabs (and indeed, all over the country) where you can satisfy your urge. If you're a high roller try the Grand Palm at the Walmont for style, while the Gaborone Sun caters for the average Joe and the Gaborone Hotel at the bus station takes any bets.

For night life there's the raunchy and risky Club Havana, with a Morris Minor on its roof next door to the Maruapula Mall in Nyerere Drive, east of the Chuma Drive intersection. The nearby Chinese and Indian restaurants look as if they might provide refuge if things get too dodgy in the club. But for the best night life in Gabs, and the whole country for that matter, drive north out of the city for 15 km to the satellite town of Phakalane. Follow the signs across the railway line, turn right at the circle and at S24° 34.168, E25° 58.466 you'll find the Fashion Lounge. This smart and glitzy nightclub occupies the entire upper floor of the Mowana Park shopping centre and hosts resident and visiting DJs, artists and bands. Entrance fees fluctuate between P30 and P50, depending on who's performing, and they also have a restaurant. Phone ahead to check the line-up on tel 350-0090.

Scottish novelist Alexander McCall Smith has put Botswana, and Gaborone in particular, on the literary map with his series of No. 1 Ladies' Detective Agency books. The fictional character of Precious Ramotswe, with her old-fashioned and morally upright outlook on life has struck a chord with 6 million readers in 36 languages. Mma Ramotswe investigates and solves delightfully traditional and mostly simple cases in and around the capital, and it is quite easy to follow in her footsteps. Zebra Way (see map) is where this 'traditionally built' lady resides; she loves to take tea and lunch at the President Hotel in the Mall, and her offices are situated in Kigale View. The love of her life, car mechanic JLB Matekoni, works on the eastern outskirts of town in Tlokweng and her ancestral village is just north of Gaborone in Mochudi. To bring these books vividly to life, join one of the guided tours mentioned at the end of this chapter.

Shopping and services

Because of the fast development of Gaborone there are few, if any, old traditional shops and shopping areas. Almost all shopping is done in the malls that are spread around the city, where you will be able to buy just about anything you might need.

As good a place to start as any is is the Game City Mall, the first mall you encounter if travelling up from the south, at the first traffic circle on entering the capital. Other than the large super-store Game, which stocks just about everything except food, there are banks, supermarkets, eateries, cinemas, hairdressers, a chemist, photo shop, internet café, bookshop and liquor store. There is also a gunsmith and outdoors shop for safari kitting-out, a bureau de change that gives good rates and an Orange mobile phone shop, in case you want to buy a local Sim card and air time for your cellphone.

Another well-stocked alternative is the River Walk Mall on the Tlokweng border road. There you will also find eateries (Primi Piatti, Nando's and Debonairs), supermarket, cinemas, bookshop, phone shop, ATMs, etc. The Liquorama liquor store here (next door to the Abyssinia Coffee House) stocks a good selection of wines. Other good malls are Westgate Mall on the Western Bypass and Fairground Mall on Machel Drive.

The Botswana Craft Centre, just off the Western Bypass, near to the intersection with Nelson Mandela Drive, offers curios, arts and crafts, some of which are made at workshops on the premises. And if it's decent wines, cigars or biltong you're after, look in at The Wine Route in Unit 6 of the centre.

Other services

Medical

For any medical emergencies, head straight to the Gaborone Private Hospital on Segoditshane Way, a continuation of Machel/Mobuto/Nyerere Drive. They are well equipped to handle most medical and dental procedures. Tel 388-5600.

Courier

For courier services, there is a choice: DHL Express, Plot 20610, Broadhurst Industrial Estate, tel 391-2000; EMS Express, Plot 60, International Commerce Park, tel 390-0963; or Botswana Couriers, Plot 22110, Kgomokasitwa Rd, tel 393-0629.

Laundry

C'est Magnifique Laundry and Dry-cleaners offers a same-day service to wash, dry and iron a basket of your dirty, dusty washing for a mere P80. They are at the Maruapula Mall in Limpopo Drive, off Chuma Drive, tel 390-8715.

Tourism

The Botswana Tourism Board is situated on the Ground Floor, Block B, Fairgrounds Office Park, Fairgrounds Estate.

EMBASSIES

- Angolan Embassy, tel 390-0204
- British High Commission, tel 395-2841
- Chinese Embassy, tel 395-2209
- Cuban Embassy, tel 391-1484
- Danish Consulate, tel 395-3505
- French Embassy, tel 395-3683
- German Embassy, tel 395-3143
- Indian High Commission, tel 397-2676
- Kenyan High Commission, tel 395-1408
- Libyan Embassy, tel 395-2481
- Namibian High Commission, tel 390-2217
- Nigerian High Commission, tel 391-3561
- South African High Commission, tel 390-4800
- Swedish Embassy, tel 395-3912
- USA Embassy, tel 395-3982
- Zambian High Commission, tel 395-1951
- Zimbabwean High Commission, tel 391-4495

Motor repairs

For vehicle repairs and maintenance:

Toyota: Motor Centre Botswana, Machel Drive, tel 395-1736

Land Rover: Lesedi Motors, Luthuli Rd, tel 391-2741

Ford and Mazda: Barloworld Motor, Haile Selassie Rd, tel 365-6000

Nissan: Broadhurst Motors, Kubu Rd, tel 391-2579

Tata: Commercial Motors, Mokolowana Rd, tel 395-2652

Jeep, Mitsubishi, Mercedes: Naledi Motors, Francistown Highway, tel 241-3602

Windscreens: Glasfit, Savute Rd, tel 350-0142

Tyres: Maxi Prest, New Lobatse Rd, tel 316-4821

24-hour breakdown service: Gaborone Towing Services, tel 391-4996

Car hire

Avis (tel 391-3093)
Budget (tel 390-2030)
Imperial (tel 390-7233)
All have counters at Gaborone International Airport.

Communications

Internet cafés are found in most malls or in Postnet outlets and Botswana post offices.

Quick fixes

Liquor is sold only in liquor stores, not in supermarkets. Car washing is offered at roadsides all over town. And if you are rushing through Gaborone on the Western Bypass, the Engen 1 Stop offers a Quickshop, Wimpy, ATM, car wash, toilets – and fuel!

Around Gaborone

The towns and villages around the capital city are steeped in the early history of the country. Tribes clashing with the Matabele and the Boers, David Livingstone and the London Missionary Society, local culture and handicrafts – it's all there.

At 50 km out of Gaborone, Molepolole is an easy excursion – take the signposted road off the Western Bypass. Just before entering Molepolole take the turn-off to Thamaga and stop in Tshanyane Kloof to see where David Livingstone spent the night in Kobokwe Cave, defying local myths that warned of evil spirits there. Or carry on into town to visit the London Missionary Church which was built in the early 1900s. Also to be seen in Molepolole is the Scottish Livingstone Memorial Hospital, one of the oldest in Botswana, and the Kgosi Sechele Museum displaying local artefacts, historical photographs and paintings.

To see more sites associated with Livingstone, take the Thamaga-Kanye turn-off from the Molepolole road. You will first pass an interesting pottery works in Pelegano village where traditional pots, jars, mugs and candlesticks are made and sold. Thamaga village also has a similar small pottery industry. On the banks of the Kolobeng River are the ruins of David Livingstone's house and mission church, built in the 1880s. The lonely grave of his daughter is also marked here. Taking the turn-off to Manyama will bring you to the Livingstone tree, a big spreading, sprawling tree believed to have been planted by the great explorer.

Situated on the north-eastern outskirts of Gaborone is the 500 sq km Gaborone Game Reserve. Run by the Department of Wildlife and National Parks, this small reserve is stocked with a good selection of animals, but no predators. It can be visited in a normal two-wheel-drive vehicle and it is popular with day visitors and picnickers (no camping). Tel 397-1405 and fees are the same as in other national parks.

Kaie Tours offers half-day and full-day tours around Gaborone, which include city tours, art and craft tours and game-viewing excursions to all the above-mentioned sites. They also do longer safaris into the Khutse Game Reserve with San guides. Contact them on tel 397-3388, e-mail safaris@kaietours.com, web www.kaietours.com. Another operation that offers similar tours is Garcin Safaris, which also runs a Mma Ramotswe tour (based on the Alexander McCall Smith books) and will handle bookings for all accommodation, flights and national parks in Botswana. Tel 393-8190, e-mail garcinsafaris@info.bw, web www.garcinsafaris.com. Africa Insight is another operation that offers Precious Ramotswe guided tours, tel 7265-4323, e-mail info@africainsight.com, web www.africainsight.com.

Eastern Botswana, Francistown and the Tuli Block

12

The two main features of eastern Botswana are the A1 route between Gaborone and Francistown, which is the main arterial highway of the country, and the Tuli Block with its farms and game reserves.

Cycle – and also horse – safaris are offered at Mashatu private game reserve, one of several private lodge operators in the North Tuli section of the Tuli Block.

Mahalapye

The A1 out of Gaborone starts as a dual carriageway and it's easy to get up a good speed, but beware of speed traps and stray animals (wild and domesticated). It's a straight and comfortable ride for 205 km to Mahalapye, the first town of any size and importance. The headquarters of Botswana Railways, with an old steam train on display, is on the right as you enter town, followed by Berak Motor Repairs and Tyre World. Then cross the traffic circle and pass a Caltex service station and shops on your left. Also on the left is the neat, tidy and conveniently situated Tshidi Guest House. There is safe parking in the yard and double chalets with bathrooms, air-con and TV cost P267. Larger en-suite doubles in the main house are P420, while breakfast costs an extra P35. Tel 471-4784.

Carrying on through town, you pass an Engen service station with a Quick Shop and take-aways, all on the left. Across the road on the right is a railway crossing and that way will take you to the Maeto Lodge. Set against a hillside is a selection of accommodation ranging from double rooms with TV, air-con and fridge for P390, to rondavels or flats for P570. Tel 472-0001, e-mail maetolodge@yahoo.com. There is also a bureau de change on the premises.

Further on through town is an FNB bank with ATM, another bureau de change, chemist, Spar supermarket and a Shell Ultra City with 24-hour ATM and shop on the way out of town. Next door to Shell is a large Toyota dealership and a nearby tyre service shop. There is also the turn-off to the Stockpoort border post and Mr Moyo's 24-hour breakdown service, tel 471-3170.

Just north of town, on the right-hand side (S23° 04.832, E26° 50.904) are the ethnically attractive rondavels of Gaetsho Lodge. With TV, air-con, fridge and coffee-making facilities, this en-suite accommodation costs P365 double (like many other establishments, the charge is the same for single and double accommodation). Contact them on tel/fax 472-0651 or mobile 7160-2322.

Palapye

Beyond Mahalapye, the countryside becomes more attractive, undulating with dense bushveld, and the road is good and wide and not so busy. Ten km south of Palapye, a road turns east towards the South African border post at Martin's Drift. To visit Palapye town, continue to the big intersection further up the road. This is an important junction as it is also the turn-off west to Serowe, Orapa and on via an all-tar road to Maun. A cluster of shops, service stations, hotels and other services has sprung up around this intersection that now rivals Palapye town centre. Engen, Spar, Woolworths, Nando's, Caltex and a tyre shop all crowd around the traffic lights here.

There is even a casino at the Cresta Botsalo Hotel. The hotel has 50 double rooms, each with air-con, satellite TV and coffee-making facilities. A double room is P880 a night. Contact them on tel 492-0245, e-mail resbotsalo@cresta.co.bw, web www.crestahosp.co.za. Another option along the same strip of road is the Desert Sands Motel with comfortable single or double rooms

Attractive riverside accommodation at the Cresta Marang Hotel welcomes weary travellers who, in Francistown, fear they're in for a rough night in this busy, industrial centre.

at P475. Tel 492-4400, e-mail ismail@ desertsandsmotel.com, web www.palapye.com/desertsandsmotel.

If you have the time and inclination to break your journey for a while, turn off the highway at this intersection and travel for 5 km down to the original Palapye for a glimpse of what the old Botswana towns looked like before the highway slashed past and changed things. Other than a well-stocked Spar shopping centre, the town boasts 2 colourful places to stay.

The first is the sprawling, faded-glory Palapye Hotel down at the railway station. Situated virtually on the station platform, it was the scene of some great parties when the train (which ran from Cape Town all the way up to the Copperbelt in Zambia and on into the Congo) used to stop here. Old sepia photographs in the atmospheric Charlie's Bar still depict scenes of 'great white' hunters, old wagon trains and fancy travellers who all passed through on their way to adventure.

With basic, but clean en-suite rooms at a mere P150 single and P200 double, and only slightly more if you want to watch Bots TV in your room, it's the bargain of the country. They'll even throw in breakfast (well, delivered on a tray actually). They're never full but if you want to phone ahead, the number is 492-0277.

The other great place to stay is Camp Itumela. It's one of those places that all the regular Africa travellers know about and use, but tell no-one about – a classic overlander's oasis (S22° 33.579, E27° 07.646). Across the tracks from the Palapye Hotel and situated in a grove of shady trees, it is well run, has a great bar and good food. There are chalets at P300 single and P380 double and a large camping area at P75 a person. They do laundry, have a communal kitchen, supply the fire and sell braai packs – what more could you want? Tel/fax 492-0228, mobile 7180-6771, e-mail campitumela @botsnet.bw, web www.palapye.com/ campitumela.

A baobab tree dominates the skyline in the Tuli Block. Dry stone wall remains on this koppie tell of an ancient culture that dominated the region around 1 300 years ago.

Tuli region

If you are arriving from SA via Martin's Drift, you might want to break your journey at the border at the very pleasant Kwa Nokeng Lodge. Set in park-like surroundings on the banks of the Limpopo River, it offers great accommodation, a bar and restaurant built on a deck over the river, swimming pool, prolific birdlife and grassy campsites. A river cottage that sleeps 4 in 2 bedrooms, air-con and a kitchen will set you back P835 a night, thatched bungalows or luxury tents on stilts over the river with en-suite bathrooms that sleep 2 adults and 2 children cost P495, safari tents sleep 2 for P245 and camping costs P70 a person. They also offer 4x4 and quad bike adventures into the Tuli Block and further afield. You'll find the place behind the Caltex service station on the left as you enter Botswana, or contact them on tel 491-5908, e-mail clinton@botsnet.bw, web www.kwanokeng.com.

About 9 km up the road towards Palapye, at the little settlement of Sherwood, is a Total garage, take-away and bureau de change. Just beyond Sherwood is the first of a number of veterinary control points where they might confiscate meat products (see page 60 for details). To enter and experience the Tuli Block, turn off right (north-east) at a sign that says Baines' Drift. A wide gravel road with a good surface will whisk you up into Botswana's most underrated tourist destination. Between 10 and 20 km wide and about 350 km from north to south, the 'block' was established by arch-colonist Cecil John Rhodes in one attempt to attach at least a part of the old Bechauanaland into his own empire (which at that stage

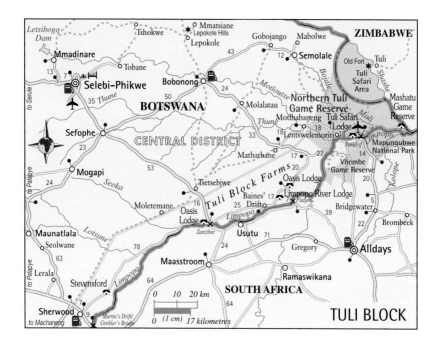

TULI BLOCK

included neighbouring Rhodesia, where you'll find the Tuli Circle).

It consists of individually owned, prime parcels of land, each with a section of Limpopo or Shashe river frontage. Most parcels have now been joined together in wildlife conservancies and, with fences down and strict ecological policies and practices in place, the region has become a viable alternative to Botswana's better-known game reserves to the north. The dominant reserve in the area is Mashatu Private Game Reserve. But with no towns, shops or petrol stations in the area, make sure you are well stocked up with fuel, food and drink.

The first accommodation you will come across is Stevensford Game Reserve, 21 km from Sherwood. Stevensford has neat bungalows around an 'out of Africa' central cook-

ing, dining and bar area, there is a reservoir to swim in and a guide to accompany you on game walks. Although they don't have any of the Big Five (except rare sightings of leopard), other game is quite plentiful and the birdlife is prolific. Campsites are set under giant trees on the river bank and offer complete privacy. Bungalows are P300 a person a day sharing, and camping P100. Tel +27-(0)83-631-3656, e-mail info@stevensfordgamereserve.com, web www.stevensfordgamereserve.com.

Further up the road at S21° 52.120, E28° 49.100 is the little-used Zanzibar border post with South Africa. Here you will find the Oasis Lodge, an attractive complex of wood, stone and thatch buildings. Rates are P450 for a luxury double suite, P450 for a double rondavel and P100 a person for camping, tel 7131-3399, e-mail info@oasislodges. co.za, web www.oasislodges.co.za.

Continue east on a gradually deteriorating dirt road for 25 km to pass the Baines' Drift police post, and another 8 km will bring you to the Limpopo River Lodge (S22° 28.959, E28° 45.503). Access is by reservation only, so enquire at reception before heading down to the river where all the accommodation is. The reserve offers a huge, unspoilt chunk of bushveld littered with koppies, mopane veld and baobabs with a good selection of antelope, elephant, leopard, cheetah and occasionally lions.

There is a network of roads, but a 4x4 is recommended. The accommodation is strung out along the river and consists mainly of 2-bedroomed chalets that sleep 4 and have wonderful views and cosy kitchen/dining/bar bomas out the back (P350 a person). Twin-bedded en-suite rondavels cost P290 and there are 7 beautiful riverside campsites that will set you back P110 a person; tel 7210-6098, e-mail limpopo@mega.bw, web www.limpoporiverlodge.co.za.

Some 5 km up the road you will reach the turn-off to another lonely border post, Platjan. The petrol station at this intersection has closed so

THE MIRACLE OF TULI

During the years that Bechuanaland was a British protectorate the Tuli was predominantly a hunting area. Hunters wiped out most of the game, and then came cattle farmers, so that by the early 1950s most wild species had become locally extinct. Fortunately, in the late 1960s, 35 far-sighted farmers ripped out their fences and proclaimed the Northern Tuli Game Reserve. With the re-introduction of many species, the free movement and natural breeding of wildlife, and good management the area is now once again host to the large herds of yesteryear.

There is even more good news in store for the animals: work is well underway to incorporate it into an extensive transfrontier park. Known as the Shashe/Limpopo Transfrontier Conservation Area, it will straddle the Limpopo and Shashe rivers to include the eastern corner of Botswana, the south-western corner of Zimbabwe and the north-eastern region of South Africa all the way to the Kruger Park (which is itself part of another, even larger Limpopo transfrontier park). An agreement was signed in June, 2006 between the ministers for environment of Botswana, South Africa and Zimbabwe in which it was agreed to jointly protect and manage the conservation area, and it is hoped that local communities as well as the wildlife will benefit greatly. The only stumbling block right now is Zimbabwe, where much of the land in question was forcibly handed over to so-called war veterans as part of the country's controversial land restitution programme. By the time you read this, however, sanity might well have returned to that country.

I hope you filled up when you last had a chance (Sherwood, if coming from the south, Bobonong from the north). There is another Oasis Lodge here. Smaller and more intimate with friendly staff, it's a most welcoming place. Double rooms with en-suite at P450 and camping is P100 a person. Tel 7273-3234, e-mail info@oasislodges. co.za, web www.oasislodges.co.za.

The road, still reasonably good gravel, continues north to the Lekkerpoort intersection, where you can swing west to leave the Tuli Block via Bobonong. But carry on straight for another 8 km to enter the Northern Tuli Game Reserve. Just as you are becoming used to looking out for the game which roams freely around here, the sight of a large irrigation farm, Talana Farms, surprises you with its cotton, maize and commercial ostriches. Here you will have to cross the wide expanse of the Motloutse River, which is a soft, sandy 4x4 riverbed in the dry season, but can turn treacherous when in flood, so avoid it then. The river is also intersected here by the amazing phenomenon of Solomon's Wall. This is a

natural dolerite dyke 30 m high which, at first appearance, looks like it was built there. The dyke would once have formed a waterfall until the river cut through it tens of millions of years ago. It's a very photogenic spot and there is also a good picnic spot on the southern bank (S22° 13.627, E28° 59.093).

Two kilometres past the river at S22° 11.591, E29° 00.533 is a poorly signposted 4-way intersection. Head straight across for the Pontdrif border post, right to Lentswe and left to Motlabaneng. Heading for Pontdrif, you'll pass through a veterinary gate, then the turn-off to Tuli Safari Lodge, the turn-off to Limpopo airfield and finally reach the border post with adjacent offices of Mashatu River Lodge. Pontdrif is the northern gateway into the Tuli and slightly less than 100 km from Musina in SA.

One of the reasons why the Tuli Block is less popular than it could be, is that this northern section is closed to the public and open only to guests of a couple of exclusive lodges. Essentially for the fly-in tourist, private vehicles are not allowed. If you

Solomon's Wall, a natural dolerite dyke cutting across the Motloutse River, resembles the work of giants long ago.

can afford the luxury and want your every need catered, then this is for you, but the northern Tuli is unfortunately not for the self-drive tourist (self-drive guests also have to leave their cars at the border and when the Limpopo is in flood they are ferried across in baskets by a suspended cableway).

Two very exciting things you can do here, however, are mountain bike and horse-back safaris in real safari style. For what you get they are extremely good value for money. The 2 operators in this area are Mashatu Lodge (which does the riding safaris from tented camps), tel 264-5321, e-mail mashatures@ malamala.com, and Tuli Safari Lodge, tel 264-5303, e-mail info@tulilodge. com, web www.tulilodge.com.

Selebi-Phikwe

Now, to get back into mainstream Botswana, head north-west from the Lekkerpoort intersection to Bobonong where you will find fuel, a bottle store and take-aways, but not much else. It's another 78 km to the large town of Selebi-Phikwe where all amenities and accommodation will be waiting for you. Entering Selebi-Phikwe from the south-east, there is a Total garage on the left and the Syringa Lodge on the right. The hotel has attractive green gardens and all rooms face onto this pleasant inner courtyard. There is also a casino and Spur steakhouse on the premises. Rates are P660 single or double and a little cheaper over weekends. Contact them on tel 261-0444.

Further into town is the Travel Inn where a standard double room is P350 and luxury double P450. A 2-bed-roomed flat that sleeps 4 costs P550 a night. Tel 262-2999, e-mail travelinn@ botsnet.bw. Another Cresta hotel, the Bosele, is in the centre of Selebi-Phikwe and is the most popular and up-market establishment in town. It has 51 air-conditioned bedrooms, a pool, business centre, conference facilities, restaurant and bars. Their well-appointed rooms cost P725 single, P892 double and they even have an all-but-forgotten camp-site around the back at P75 a person. Tel 261-0675, e-mail resbosele@cresta. co.bw, web www.crestahosp.co.za.

The main thoroughfare through Selebi-Phikwe is Tshekedi Road where you'll find banks, ATMs, supermarkets, a butchery and petrol stations. The (unsignposted) way out of town towards Serule and the A1 is past the police station and post office. Conveniently situated on the way out is the inexpensive, but clean, Phikwe Guest House where en-suite single or double costs P200 including breakfast! Small and simple in a converted residential home, they also have safe off-street parking. Tel 261-0834, e-mail koyobo2003@yahoo.com.

Selebi-Phikwe owes its existence to copper and nickel mines in the area, which make it quite prosperous. This has spawned a large industrial area on the outskirts of town where most mechanical repairs and maintenance can be done.

Bamangwato Toyota is in Meepo Road and can be reached on tel 261-0539; Boiteko Metal Products do repairs to trailers, panel beating and welding, tel 261-4076; DHL is on 262-2715; Maxi Prest Tyres are in Pope John Paul Road, tel 261-0511; and Motovac for auto parts in Borakanelo Road on tel 261-4169. For

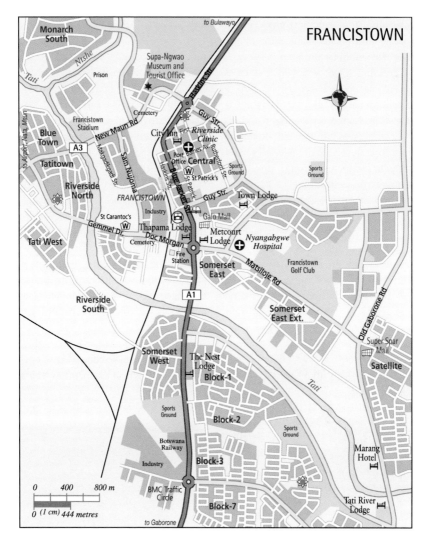

medical emergencies phone the government hospital ambulance on 261-0997.

Francistown

Botswana's main south–north highway, the A1, is joined at Serule where there is a Shell garage situated just shy of a railway line (look out for trains that do run on this line). Another 85 km north on the A1 will bring you to the second-largest city in Botswana, Francistown. Established during a short-lived gold rush in the 1860s, it is now a thriving, mostly industrial city serving as the gateway to the north and also Zimbabwe. With good accommodation and shops on the banks of the pretty Tati River, Francistown is a popular place to stop over and stock up in before heading into the wilds of the northern safari circuit.

Entering town, you will first cross over the BMC traffic circle with a Shell garage on the left. Next up is the Nest Lodge on the right and an industrial area on the left. Roadside entrepreneurs repair silencers and exhaust systems along this section as you pass through a couple of traffic lights. After you cross the Tati River there is a large Engen garage, a Wimpy and Spar supermarket on the left and a Mitsubishi garage on the right. At the next circle you can turn left to travel to Nata, straight ahead for the Cresta Thapama Hotel and the town centre, and right for the Cresta Marang Hotel and Tati River Lodge.

Where to stay in Francistown

Conveniently situated on the right as you enter the city is the safe, secure and value-for-money Nest Lodge. Each room has a TV and refrigerator and costs only P300 single and P350 double – breakfast is an extra P50 a person. Contact them on tel 242-0100. The next establishment you reach (if arriving from the south) is the recently refurbished, up-market Cresta Thapama Hotel and Casino, which you will find at the town's main traffic circle. Marketed as the top hotel in town, this large 4-star hotel has 96 spacious air-conditioned rooms, a business centre with free internet, swimming pool, restaurant and cocktail bar (2 for the price of 1 at happy hour). The casino is packed with optimists every night and they also have a well-equipped gym and 2 squash courts. Room rates are P982 single and P1 205 double. Tel 241-3872, e-mail resthapama@cresta.co.bw, web www.crestahosp.co.za.

If you turn right at the main city traffic circle and travel for 5 km along the old Gaborone road, you'll reach my favour-

There is a good selection of more-than-comfortable campsites in the Tuli Block, like this one at the Limpopo River Lodge, as well as reasonably priced game lodges.

Bus routes fan out in all directions from the busy bus station in Francistown. Although seldom used by tourists, public transport in Africa is a highly underrated option.

ite place to stay in Francistown, the Cresta Marang Hotel (S21° 11.851, E27° 2.074). Built alongside the Tati River, it is all gleaming wood, thatched roofs and attentive staff. The gardens are lush, the lawns green, the pool sparkles and its bar has draft beer – what more could you ask for? Rooms range from quaint chalets on stilts near the river and comfortable bungalows to the new motel-styled residency. But they all cost the same: P850 single and P1000 double. A full buffet breakfast costs P95. The best part is that all this is available to campers who pay only P60 a person to camp in these beautiful surroundings. Tel 241-3991, e-mail resmarang@cresta.co.bw, web www.crestahosp.co.za.

A little further down the road and across the river is the Tati River Lodge. Laid out like a small village behind a high security fence, which unfortunately cuts residents off from the river, they are a bit plainer and cheaper than their neighbours. Rates are P600 single, P700 double and P50 a person camping. Tel 240-6000, e-mail res@trl.co.bw, web www.trl.co.bw.

Back at the main traffic circle again, opposite the Cresta Thapama Hotel on Blue Jacket Street, is the newly renovated Metcourt Lodge. It is a neat, compact, African-chic 3-star hotel in the centre of town offering all the services a businessman or tourist should need, including a Spur steakhouse on the premises. Rates are P612 a night, single or double and exclude breakfast. Tel 244-1100, e-mail info@ft.metcourt.com, web www.metcourt.com.

At the top of Blue Jacket Street (love that name!) and two blocks on in Khama Street, is the City Inn. Really a converted shopping mall but comfortable and quiet, it has 16 en-suite rooms with fridge and TV for P400 single and P450 double. No phone, no pool, no pets, but there is a Taste of India restaurant across the way. Contact the Inn on tel 244-2199.

Shopping and eating in Francistown

Like Gaborone, Francistown has been 'malled' by many new shopping centres. On the way out to the Cresta Marang Hotel you'll pass a big SuperSpar and mall. This Spar is well stocked and there is also a bottle store, internet café and laundry in the mall. Most of Francistown's shops are up Blue Jacket Street, beyond the Cresta Thapama Hotel. There you will find another Spar, Shoprite supermarket, KFC take-aways, FNB bank and a bureau de change.

One block east along Blue Jacket Street is Galo Mall with the town's largest variety of shops and services. There is a Pick 'n Pay supermarket, Woolworths, bank, ATM, Nando's, CNA, Cape Union Mart, chemist, bottle store, Hard Rock Café and the usual range of SA clothing shops.

For the hungry and thirsty there's a selection of fast-food outlets attached to service stations and in the shopping malls. Or if you have the time and want the added comfort, try the bars and restaurants at the Thapama or Marang hotels, the Spur at the Metcourt or the Hard Rock Café at the Galo Mall.

Medical

More importantly for some will be the doctor's and dental surgery upstairs at Lordsland Medical Centre – open Mon to Fri, 08h00 to 17h30 and Sat, 08h00 to 13h00. Tel 7169-1922. For serious accidents and 24-hour medical emergencies, rush to Riverside Clinic

in the northern section of town at Plot 424, Baines' Ave. (S21° 09.796, E27° 030.762), tel 241-2518 or 241-6017.

Motor and related

Francistown Toyota is just over the railway bridge on the Nata-Maun road, tel 241-3855. Barloworld Motor is up the road in Sam Nujoma Drive for Ford and Mazda, tel 241-2323. Francistown Nissan is in the industrial area, tel. 241-2380, and Lesedi Motors will look after your Land Rover, tel 241-6601. Francistown Panel Beaters, in the industrial area, will tow you in and repair your vehicle in the unfortunate event of an accident, tel 241-2722. Maxi Prest will sort your tyres out in Sam Nujoma Drive, tel 241-4502. PG Glass for windscreens is in Gemsbok Street, tel 241-6476 and – I love this – The Jolly Bushman in Dumela Industrial Area fixes tents and sells camping equipment. If you can master the phonetic clicks, phone him on 241-6624.

Leaving town

All roads out of Francistown radiate from the traffic circle at the bottom end of Blue Jacket Street. North on the A1 takes you 83 km to the Zimbabwean border at Plumtree; south takes you back down to Gaborone, and west will lead you to Nata and from there on to Maun or Kasane (but be careful of the ridiculous 60kph speed limits along sections of this road). The bus station is close to the circle too, just behind the Cresta Thapama Hotel, and the airport is out on the Nata road. Air Botswana has offices there (tel 241-2393) as does Avis Rent-a-Car (tel 241-3901).

Nata and the Makgadikgadi Pans 13

For many travellers, this is the gateway to the wonderful wild north. Cities and the tame towns are left behind, the camping gear can be put to proper use and there's the chance to use a 4×4 – and get stuck.

Guests enjoy a refreshing swim at the aptly named Planet Baobab after a dusty day on the pans. The 'Planet' is a fairly new body near Gweta, on the Nata-Maun orbit.

In this chapter I have included Sowa, Ntwetwe, and Nxai pans as well as the 2 towns that serve them, Nata and Gweta. Sowa (sometimes spelt Sua) and Ntwetwe pans are collectively known as the Makgadikgadi Pans and cover a vast area of 12 000 sq km. Once part of a huge inland sea, these (mostly) dry, flat pans now offer isolation, inaccessibility, beauty and danger – a heady mix. Don't tackle them lightly. Come well equipped with sufficient water, food and fuel, have good maps and knowledge, travel with at least 1 other vehicle as backup and stay away during wet times: there is a rainy season, but unseasonal rains are not unknown. If you get stuck on the pans, it might take days to get out and you might ruin more than just your holiday plans. People have lost vehicles and trailers there for good where the thin salt crust conceals a deep pit of salt sludge.

Nata

If you leave Francistown on the A3 it's only 232 km of good tarred road to Nata. However, you should make the time and effort to turn in at the Nata Bird Sanctuary 20 km before you reach the town – and it's really not so much of a town as a cluster around an intersection. You don't have to be a bird lover to appreciate and use the facilities here as it affords you the chance to ride across a large section of the pans and even camp there. But if you are a keen birder, you'll appreciate that it has been designated an Important Bird Area (IBA) and as such is one of Botswana's premier birding destinations.

After good rains, thousands of globally threatened lesser flamingos,

greater flamingos, chestnut-banded plovers, great white and pink-backed pelicans among a host of water birds converge on the nutrient-rich waters of the pans. A viewing platform has been erected 10 km from the gate, on the edge of the pan – just beware of the danger of getting stuck after heavy rains! A comprehensive checklist of birds found in the sanctuary can be found on the BirdLife Botswana web site www.birdlifebotswana.org.bw and you are encouraged to enter your own bird list in Botswana Tickbird, a web-based bird monitoring system at www.worldbirds.org/botswana.

Camping, with hot showers and flush toilets, is provided in a shaded mopane woodland near the entrance gate. Entrance costs P75 a person and P20 a vehicle, while camping costs P50 a person. The sanctuary is open every day from 07h00 to 19h00, but enquire about road conditions at the entrance gate, as you might need a 4×4.

The ever-popular Nata Lodge is another 10 km further up the road and offers chalets, luxury tents, a welcoming bar and restaurant that overlooks the swimming pool, camping, quad bike trails and pan trips. A comfortable stop-over on the way to just about anywhere in northern Bots (Chobe and Ngamiland districts), Nata Lodge can become crowded, so it's wise to book ahead in peak times. Twin chalets cost P630 a night, family chalets sleep four and cost P720, a 2-bed en-suite tent P525 and camping is P60 a person. Tel 620-0070, e-mail reservations@natalodge.com, web www.natalodge.com.

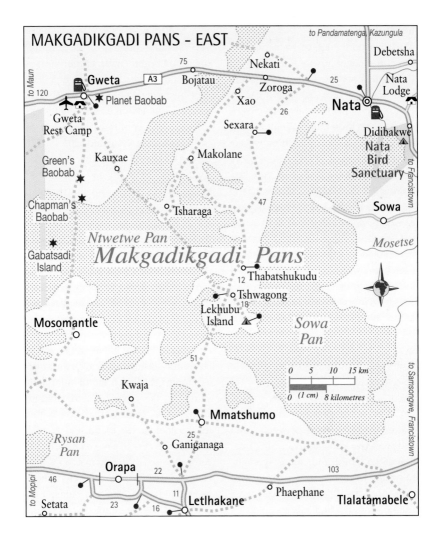

MAKGADIKGADI PANS - EAST

to Pandamatenga, Kazungula

Debetsha

to Maun

Gweta A3 Bojatau

75 Nekati

Zoroga

25 Nata Lodge

to 120

Planet Baobab

Xao

26

Nata

Gweta Rest Camp

Sexara

Didibakwe

Green's Baobab

Kauxae

Makolane

Nata Bird Sanctuary

to Francistown

Chapman's Baobab

Tsharaga

47

Sowa

Ntwetwe Pan

Mosetse

Gabatsadi Island

Makgadikgadi Pans

12 Thabatshukudu

Tshwagong

Lekhubu Island

18

Sowa Pan

Mosomantle

51

to Samsongwe, Francistown

0 5 10 15 km

0 (1 cm) 8 kilometres

Kwaja

Mmatshumo

Rysan Pan

25 Ganiganaga

Orapa

22

103

46

to Mopipi

Setata 23 11 Letlhakane 16 Phaephane Tlalatamabele

On entering Nata town you will cross the bridge over the Nata River and pass the police station on your left. Further on, also on the left, is an Engen garage with take-aways and a small shop, then a Shell garage. Between the 2 is 3-Way Recovery (tel 7244-7735) for an emergency breakdown service. Across the road, opposite the turn-off to Maun, is a new Shell garage with a well-stocked 24-hour shop selling groceries, take-aways and booze. It is owned by 'Mr Nata', Seloma Tiro, who also owns the adjoining Northgate Lodge with rooms, chalets and restaurant. Double chalets are P400 and big double rooms with air-con and TV are P600. Tel 621-1108.

Lekhubu

The road north out of Nata runs for 300 km straight up to Kazungula on Botswana's northeastern border. From here you can turn off right to enter Zimbabwe, or take the ferry that crosses the Zambezi River there to enter Zambia (see page 144). But right now we are heading west out of Nata to explore the pans. If you make it to only one destination on Makgadikgadi, it has to be Lekhubu Island (previously known as Kubu). Surrounded by the treacherous sands of Sowa Pan, this cluster of huge boulders and even bigger baobab trees rises like a mirage. To see it bathed in moonlight or kissed by a sunrise or sunset is an unforgettable sight (at full moon you get sunset and moonrise at the same time). Lekhubu is one of those spectacular, difficult-to-reach spots in southern Africa that makes you proud to be able to say 'I've been there'.

In theory it should be easy to find Lekhubu – just head south off the main Nata-Maun road between Sowa and Ntwetwe pans and you can't miss it. But you can, and almost certainly would with this approach, so zero your tripmeter at the Nata intersection, charge your GPS and let's go.

Your first turn-off option is at 17.6 km (S20° 10.677, E26° 01.336) where there is a signpost announcing 'Kubu Island 95.1 km'. That way down is often flooded and you might have to continue along the Maun road to the 26-km mark (S20° 10.028, E25° 56.890) where there is another indistinct and unmarked turn-off south. This track crosses the old gravel Maun road and continues for 26.5 km

to a cattle post (S20° 18.705, E25° 48.290). The countryside is beautiful open grassland with cattle, horses and large birds like korhaans and kori bustards. Another 47 km brings you to Thabatshukudu village. Pass through and continue for 10 km to the Tshwagong vet gate (S20° 45.820, E25° 44.317). After another 2 km the road forks: keep left and you should see Lekhubu 8 km down this road. With the island so tantalisingly close, it's tempting to rush across the open section of pan. But beware: don't venture further if the pan has water on it, or is even damp, as it could give way.

The island is under the management of Mmatshumo village and there is a fee of P75 a person, P50 a vehicle and P50 to camp. The island's isolation and the difficulty in finding it and getting there, create the feeling of having arrived on a pilgrimage. The mystical aura that surrounds the grotesque and fantastic shapes of the baobabs that grow out of the boulder-strewn island add to that feeling. Needless to say, you need to be completely self-sufficient in a tough 4×4 vehicle, treat the place with the utmost respect and carry out all your litter.

If you are heading south from here, you can leave the pans via Mmatshumo and continue south to Serowe, or head east to Francistown. From the island you can head southwest across the pans only if conditions are bone-dry, otherwise head back for 8 km in a north-westerly direction, to join the road just south of the Tshwagong vet gate, turn south for 29 km to another vet gate (S20° 58.618, E25° 37.180) and it's another

22 km to Mmatshumo. Just 25 km more takes you to the tarred road between Orapa and Francistown, or another 13 km south will bring you to the road to Serowe.

Planet Baobab and Gweta

If you're still stuck up on the main Nata-Maun road looking for the turn-off south to Lekhubu, rather give up and shoot on through to Gweta, 100 km from Nata. About 4 km before Gweta there's a turn-off south to funky Planet Baobab – you can't miss it as there's a large planet balanced on a termite mound at the spot S20° 11.059, E25° 18.004. Planet Baobab offers accommodation in Afro-eccentric rondavels decorated in chic and colourful style, or shaded campsites.

You can't miss the Planet Baobab turn-off, a favourite landmark on the A3 near Gweta.

There is a sparkling pool to cool down in and a welcoming bar decorated with old *Drum* magazine (the magazine of choice for many Africans during apartheid-era South Africa) photographs and Africa-themed movie posters. The chandeliers are made from empty beer bottles and the patio chairs are covered with Nguni cowhide (the now much fancied breed of indigenous cattle). There is also a dining area where they serve good, reasonably priced meals – and all is brooded over by huge, tentacled baobab trees. Through the Kalahari Surf Club they also offer activities such as village tours and quadbike safaris across the pans with overnight camping under the stars. Double rondavels cost P850 and camping is P75 a person. Tel 241-2277, e-mail reservations@unchartedafrica.com, web www.unchartedafrica.com.

Another option is to turn off at the Shell shop and garage and drive 4 km into Gweta village. There you'll find a small general dealer, a big, new government clinic and the old, established Gweta Lodge. It's a bit run-down now that the road to Maun is so much better and faster, but in days past it was a real oasis for travellers. It is still capable of throwing a good party, though. They offer rides to the pans by 4×4s or quadbikes and accommodation in rooms and bungalows. Single rooms are P320 a night, doubles P460 and camping is P50 a person. Tel 621-2220, e-mail gwetalodge@info.bw, web www.gwetalodge.com.

Ntwetwe Pan

If you didn't manage to get to Lekhubu, then try to visit some of the clusters of famous baobabs in the area of Ntwetwe Pan. Although also quite difficult to find and a tough 4×4 bundu-bash, Green's Baobab and the nearby Chapman's Baobab are fascinating markers along the routes of those early travellers. The two landmarks are best approached from Gweta, and the ideal spot to start is at Gweta Lodge. Head south-west away from the lodge for 1.3 km to a fork in the road (S20° 12.520, E25° 15.478), keep left here (right goes to the Makgadikgadi Pans National Park) and continue south for another 17 km to a confusing cluster of huts and kraals.

Press through to find the track again on the other side where it becomes narrower and overgrown (you will probably scratch the paintwork on your vehicle). Beware too of grass seeds clogging your vehicle's radiator and smouldering on the exhaust. The track can be very indistinct at times and a good sense of direction is necessary for another 8 km, to reach the spot at S20° 25.519, E25° 13.878 where you should spot a cluster of palm trees to the east that marks the close proximity of Green's Baobab (S20° 25.509, E25° 13.867). Continue south for another 10 km to S20° 30.286, E25° 12.483 where you must turn east for 3 km to reach Chapman's Baobab (S20° 29.384, E25° 14.964). To keep travelling south from here would eventually bring you to the Francistown-Orapa-Mopipi-Maun road.

Makgadikgadi Pans

There are two official entry gates into the Makgadikgadi Pans National Park. The northern one is off the main Nata-Maun road, 42 km west of Gweta and

> **GREAT MIGRATIONS**
>
> The Makgadikgadi Pans area is home to what many claim is the second-largest migration of game in Africa. During the 1960s it was estimated that 60 000 Burchell's zebra and a similar number of wildebeest trekked annually between the Boteti River in the west and the grasslands east of Gweta. They would spend the dry winter months grazing around the permanent water of the Boteti, and migrate east every year looking for the new grass brought on by summer rains.
>
> The onset of winter would see them heading west once more; a timeless cycle. Droughts, extensive veterinary fences for foot-and-mouth disease control and hunting have – there is no better word – slaughtered these animals, to an to an estimated 15 000 zebra and 3 500 wildebeest that currently make the migration. Yet it is still believed to be the second-largest after Serengeti.

163 km east of Maun. Turn south at S20° 16.895, E24° 56.172 for 5 km and then east for another 5 km to reach the game scout camp that is the entry point. The western entrance is off the Motopi-Rakops road at S20° 28.230, E24° 30.542. This is 58 km south of Motopi and 73 km north of Rakops. Turn east here to cross the normally dry Boteti River – the park boundry – to the scout camp on the other side. Here you'll find Khumaga, one of the park's two public campsites.

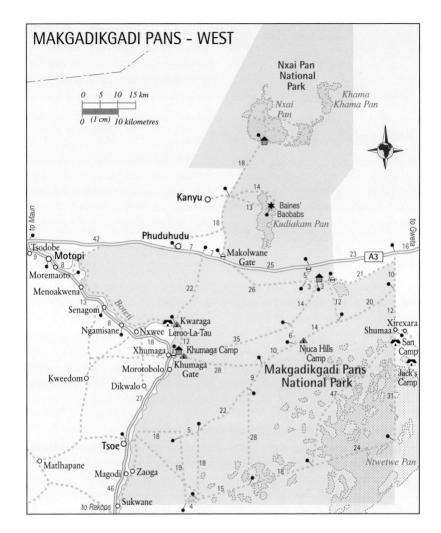

MAKGADIKGADI PANS - WEST

0 5 10 15 km

0 (1 cm) 10 kilometres

Nxai Pan
National
Park

Khama
Khama Pan

Nxai
Pan

to Maun

Kanyu ○

18

14

13

★ Baines'
Baobabs
Kudiakam Pan

18

Phuduhudu

42

○ 7

7

Makolwane
Gate

25

23 A3

16

to Gweta

Tsodobe ○
9 ○ Motopi
8

Moremaoto

Menoakwena

22

26

5
3

3

21

10

13

Senagom ○

Boteti

14

12

20

12

8

Ngamisane ●

○Nxwee

18

12

▲ Kwaraga
Leroo-La-Tau

35

6

14

Shumaa ○

Xirexara
● San
Camp

Xhumaga

▲ Khumaga Camp

10

▲ Njuca Hills
Camp

Kweedom ○

Morotobolo ○
Dikwalo ○

Khumaga
Gate

28

9

**Makgadikgadi Pans
National Park**

47

Jack's
Camp

27

31

22

Tsoe ○

18

5

28

24

Ntwetwe Pan

○ Matlhapane

Magodi ○ ○ Zaoga

46

18

18

18

to Rakops ○ Sukwane

15

4

The camp overlooks the Boteti and has basic ablution facilities.

The other public campsite is Njuca Hills, 40 km to the east at S20° 26.365, E24° 50.886. The hills offer great views of the surrounding countryside, but ablutions are even more basic with no water available. It is difficult to find some of the roads in this park as they either wash away with the annual flooding, or become overgrown. Take great care and stick to the tracks (see above). Of course, you must be totally self-sufficient to venture into this park and preferably travel in convoy with at least one other vehicle.

Nxai Pan

Botswana's most famous group of baobabs, Baines' Baobabs, lies north

Quadbikes can be hired from the lodges around Gweta for exciting guided excursions onto the pans.

of the Nata-Maun main road within the Nxai Pan National Park. To reach the park and these baobabs, drive 67 km west of Gweta to S20° 13.683, E24° 38.941 where there is a wide, sandy multi-track heading north. Just on 18.5 km of deep sand will bring you to a turn-off east (S20° 04.224, E24° 40.323), which is signposted to the place. Turn in here and, if it is the wet season, take the left fork after 1 km. This is a longer way around, but avoids having to cross waterlogged pans to get to the site. If it is dry, carry on straight and after another 12 km you will be crossing the pans directly in front of the famous historic site of Baines' Baobabs (S20° 06.739, E24° 46.147).

Thomas Baines (the artist-explorer, not to be confused the Cape's master road-builder Thomas Bain, son of the soldier-engineer Andrew Geddes) painted this scene in 1862 and it is to this day visually unchanged – baobabs (not diamonds) are forever here. There is a public campsite (same rates and

booking procedure as Nxai Pan) (See page 57) across the pan from Baines' Baobabs on a small island. The area can be visited on a day trip from Maun or Gweta and there is a nice picnic spot at the trees, but beware of snakes, leave no litter and do not park your vehicle within the root area of the trees.

Retracing your tracks 13 km back to the main sand road, turn north and drive for another 18 km to the entrance gate of Nxai Pan (S19° 56.046, E24° 45.719). If you have booked and prepaid, your documentation will be checked here or you will have to hope that there is a campsite available. Entrance is P120 a day for adults, P60 for children between the ages of 8 and 17, P50 for vehicles, while camping is another P150. To reach the campsite, turn right as you pass through the gate and it is 1.5 km to the smart new ablution block. Sites are shady and water taps are set deep inside solid stone cairns to protect them from thirsty elephants.

There is the usual network of squiggly roads all over the park, few of which are signposted, so use your navigational skills with the map supplied in this chapter. There is a good variety of game, including elephants and all the predators, as well as good birding, but their presence is highly seasonal. Game will come to you if you wait at the waterholes in the dry winter season, but long grass and plentiful water will make it less easy after the summer rains.

It is 37 km of deep sand back to the main Nata-Maun road, then another 138 km of good tarmac west to Maun.

Maun and the Okavango Delta 14

For many, indeed most, visitors Maun is 'ground zero' for Botswana. Centrally situated within Ngamiland district, it's within striking distance of most of the country's top tourist spots. Locals pronounce it more like 'Maung'. It is the jumping-off place for the Delta, but also your last food, fuel and drinks stop before the wilds of Moremi, Savuti and Chobe in the north-east. It's where you head for after the dry heat of Makgadikgadi Pans and a stepping stone to Drotsky's Caves, Tsodilo Hills and the Panhandle to the north-west. In short, you can't miss it.

A male red lechwe bounds through shallow flood-plain waters of the Okavango Delta. These semi-aquatic antelope are synonymous with the permanently inundated areas.

Maun

Established in the early 20th century by the Batswana tribe, Maun aptly means 'place of reeds'. Traders, hunters and assorted adventurers drifted in and slowly the safari business started to grow – first for hunting, then for game viewing and photography. In the 1970s it was still a dusty African village with a dirt airstrip and, as its safari heart, Riley's corrugated-iron hotel and Riley's garage next door with its single hand-operated pump. They were prob-

ably the iconic landmarks of adventure travel in southern Africa. People called the Delta 'the swamps' and from there right to the heart of the Okavango was unbroken wilderness.

By the late 1980s Maun was bursting at the seams with overlanders and self-drivers, until the government changed its tourism policy in parks to encourage more expensive fly-in visitors and bring down the numbers of budget travellers. With a result Maun is more sedate now than it was 10 or 20 years

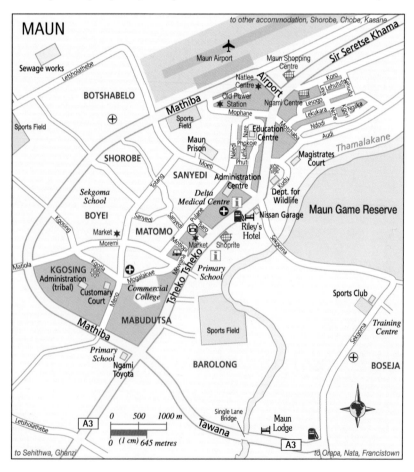

ago, and much more developed, and most tourists just change planes at the international airport.

The town is the administrative centre for Ngamiland, but gone is the wild-west atmosphere with sunburnt hunters swapping yarns at the Duck Inn, battered 4×4s and even more battered drivers. That's all been replaced by the upmarket chic of new, multi-tiered game-viewing vehicles chauffeured by smartly dressed game guides. Not the same place at all!

Getting there

Being so centrally situated, Maun can be approached from all directions. From Nata in the east (described in the previous chapter) is probably the busiest and most commercial route. A new route, gaining in popularity now that it is tarred all the way, is the road via Serowe and Rakops. This way affords shorter, quicker access from the Johannesburg/Pretoria region, up the N1 to Mokopane (Potgietersrus), then north on the N11 to the border at Martin's Drift. From there across the A1 at Palapye and on to Serowe, north-west past Orapa and on to Rakops and finally north to join the A3 at Motopi and on into Maun.

From the south-west, the Trans-Kalahari Highway links with Ghanzi and then on up through Sehithwa (where the road from Shakawe joins it) to Maun. All the above routes are tarred and easy to drive. However, if you want to approach Maun from the north-east, you'd better have a 4×4. This is the safari route from Kasane through the game reserves of Chobe and Moremi. The

tracks are sandy and rough and often blocked by deep, muddy water channels. Oh please, Botswana Government, don't ever improve it, 'cause this is the real reason why tourists drive up this way – to feel the achievement of conquering the tough conditions and seeing the game with a deeper sense of appreciation than that afforded by convenient fly-in safaris.

Coming to Maun from the east along the A3 you will spot your first accommodation, Mokoro Lodge, on the right 4 km out. A little further is the turn-off left to Lesedi Motors (Land Rover dealership) tel 686-1694, then you will spot Maxi Prest tyres and Exact Exhausts. Also on the left is a Caltex garage at the first turn-off into Maun. A Shell garage and the Maun Lodge is down this way before you cross the old single-laned bridge across the Thamalakane River (the main channel flowing south out of the Delta). If you did not turn off into Maun at the Caltex garage, you would soon reach a new Engen garage at the main road into Maun. A new bypass is under construction here that will whisk you up past Maun to the traffic circle north of town, on towards Shorobe village (where the tar ends), the 'buffalo fence' gate and eventually South Gate which is the entrance to Moremi Wildlife Reserve.

By air

The airport in Maun is one of the busiest, by flight numbers, in southern Africa. Light planes buzz in and out throughout the day, flying guests into isolated camps or doing scenic flights over the Delta. Air Botswana has direct

The hard-working fleet of light aircraft that serves lodges and camps of the Delta lines up at Maun airport. Just 35 years ago it was a case of 'beyond here be dragons'.

daily return flights to Gaborone, leaving at different times on different days. There are also direct daily return flights to Johannesburg, leaving Maun at 14h30 and arriving in Joburg at 16h30. Contact their office at Maun airport on tel 686-0762, or check the web site www.airbotswana.co.bw for latest schedules.

Air Namibia flies on Mondays, Wednesdays, Fridays and Sundays from Windhoek at 10h45 to arrive at Maun at 12h30. The flight continues on to arrive at Victoria Falls in Zimbabwe at 13h50, returns to Maun at 15h40 and eventually makes it back to Windhoek by 17h25. Web www.airnamibia.com.na.

Public transport

Buses start leaving the area around the market in Tsaro Street (opposite Nando's) from daybreak every morning and continue departing throughout the day. They head for Francistown (7 hrs), Ghanzi (4 hrs) and Shakawe (5 hrs). Ask locally for the latest fares, as fuel price increases have had a marked effect.

Getting around

Maun has grown in a haphazard fashion along the banks of the Thamalakane River and its streets have little planning or design to them. It has two main focus areas: the first is a cluster of shops, market and public transport in the south, around Riley's Hotel; the other is in the northern section of town where shops, restaurants and service industries have grown up in the area around the airport. To get a feel for the place, enter Maun across the first (single-lane) bridge and join the town's main road at the intersection that boasts the big dealership of Ngami Toyota. Turn right here and pass Tyre Vision and a pharmacy on your right with a Caltex garage and Choppies supermarket on your left.

After passing the post office on your left you reach an area of market, bus station and taxi ranks, also to your left. Shoprite is on your right and across the road is a tight cluster of Woolworths, Spar, bureau de change, Nando's, a pharmacy and the Delta Medical

Centre. Next up on your right is a Postnet with internet connection, then Riley's garage, bottle store and hotel.

To reach Maun's second centre, pass the Nissan dealership and cross over the next traffic circle. Sir Seretse Khama Road carries you north towards more shops and offices. Along the way Mophane Avenue turns off left to the old power station district (once the locale of legendary rave parties) and next is Airport Avenue (also left) which goes to the airport and offices of some of the local safari operators. Just past the airport turn-off are 2 shopping centres that face each other across the road. On the left is the Maun Shopping Centre with an outdoor equipment shop, restaurant, bottle store and Engen garage. Across from here, at Ngami Centre is the popular Spar supermarket, First National Bank and bureau de change. Beyond this area lies most of the accommodation and camps ranged along the river bank and then the road continues on to Moremi, Savuti and Chobe.

Where to stay

Instead of listing Maun's accommodation establishments in order of expense or luxury, I think it makes sense to list them in sequence as you would find them coming in from Nata and heading out towards Moremi.

Approaching Maun, 4 kilometres out on the A3, is the neat Mokoro Lodge. Built in classic (if somewhat inappropriate for these parts) motel-style, with individual parking in front of each door and 24-hour security, all 28 spacious rooms are self-catering with microwave, fridge, wash-up, cutlery and crockery.

They also have complimentary tea and coffee and a TV. It is quiet and peaceful with no bar or restaurant, and they charge P340 single and P400 double. Tel 686-0551 or 7175-2728.

Turn left at the next Caltex garage into Tawana Road and, just before the single-lane bridge across the Thamalakane River, you will find Maun Lodge. Attractively situated on a bank of the river, they offer luxury air-conditioned hotel accommodation, chalets and conference facilities. The Pygmy Goose Bar is a popular rendezvous spot and the restaurant is one of the best in Maun, offering traditional and international cuisine. Tours, safaris and scenic flights can be arranged on your behalf. Single rooms cost P810, doubles P850, double chalets P604 and family chalets (sleep 4) P750. Tel 686-3939, e-mail maun.lodge@info.bw, web www.maunlodge.com.

Riley's Hotel is the only accommodation establishment in the centre of town and also the oldest. Started from a single tin rondavel in 1910 by Harry Riley, it has developed through the years into a top modern hotel that is now the pride of the Cresta group. A new wing with luxury rooms has been built around the old historic core that still houses Harry's Bar and The Butcher's Block restaurant. Room rates are P773 single and P805 double. Tel 686-0302, e-mail resrileys@cresta.co.bw, web www.crestahosp.co.za.

Heading north on Sir Seretse Khama Road, away from the town centre, we find most of Maun's accommodation. The first up is Sedia Hotel, well signposted and set in large grounds that stretch down to the river. A popular spot with the local safari fraternity, it has a cosy bar, pool tables, and a restaurant serving value-for-money pizzas and burgers. It's a popular weekend venue for families too, with a swimming pool and kiddies playground. The quiet campsite is huge with clean ablutions and shaded sites. Solid, spacious one-bedroomed chalets cost P860 and P1070 for 2 bedrooms (B&B). Double rooms cost P650 and camping only P50 a person. Tel 686-0177. Sedia is also the headquarters of Afro Trek Safaris, which offers day trips into Moremi, scenic flights over the Delta and 2-day *mokoro* safaris. Tel/fax 686-2574.

At the end of Sir Seretse Khama Road, where it bends to the right to cross the river by the new bridge, is a turn-off left which takes you for 2 km through lush riverine forest to Island Safari Lodge (S19° 55.483, E23° 30.519). It was the second in the area, built by ex-hunter Tony Graham in the early 1970s. Set in lovely gardens, this old, established camp has been kept in fine condition and boasts spacious old-style bungalows, a bar, pool, restaurant and a quiet campsite at the river's edge. Bed and breakfast rates are P480 single, P734 double and P38 a person camping. Contact them on tel 686-0300, e-mail enquire@africansecrets.net, web www.africansecrets.net.

If you were to turn right just before the new bridge, you would meander down to another older camp, Maun Rest Camp. Owned and run by 'old hands' Simon Paul and Joyce Bestelink, it is a quiet, spotlessly clean, well-maintained and no-nonsense oasis where you can rest up and sort out before or after a hectic safari. There is no bar or restaurant and the terraced campsites overlook the river. They offer a self-catering, 4- or 6-bedded cottages at P375 a night for the first person and thereafter P75 a person. Double furnished tents are P330 and camping costs P50 a person. They also personally guide affordable photographic safaris. Tel/fax 686-3472, e-mail simonjoyce@info.bw.

Turning immediately right after you cross the new bridge will bring you to The Old Bridge Backpackers, the grooviest camp in town (S19° 56.676, E23° 29.322). David and Helena run a lovely, laid-back operation that attracts the town's most interesting characters. The music is smooth, the beers cold, the pool table abused and dishes like warthog stew are on the menu. It's situated in one of the most attractive, picturesque spots in Maun, right on the Thamalakane River, with a view off the original old pole bridge. Kids fish with home-made poles, competing with fish eagles and kingfishers, jacanas hop daintily on the lily pads and, when the water level is high, boat trips depart from here for the Delta. Accommodation is limited to camping (P45 a person), dorm beds (P132) and erected tents (P198 single and P298 double). They also offer budget mobile safaris, boat trips and can organise

---

There are two horse safari outfits in the Delta, allowing you to get right among the herds and cross deep water. The joy of riding a horse in the game-filled wilderness is hard to beat.

30 years ago you would have seen some dusty tracks, mud and grass huts and some iron bungalows. But Maun has grown into an important, modern regional centre.

scenic flights. Tel/fax 686-2406, e-mail thebridge@botsnet.bw, web www. maun-backpackers.com.

Back at the new bridge you'll find a traffic circle. Turning left here will lead you to 4 more camps, all along the river, and eventually all the way to Moremi. First up is Audi Camp with 4 luxury en-suite tents on raised wooden decking overlooking the river (P530 double, P460 single), 10 furnished and serviced tents (P330 double, P260 single), 8 dome tents with beds, but no bedding provided (P148 double, P120 single) and camping at P50 a person. This is a large and well-established operation with a restaurant and bar, swimming pool, and good security. They also offer safaris and *mokoro* trips into the Delta. Tel 686-0599, e-mail info@okavangocamp.com, web www.okavangocamp.com.

Next along is Crocodile Camp, a similar operation with a lovely bar/ restaurant built out on poles over the river. This was the original family home of the Wilmots, the patriarch of whom

was the famous crocodile hunter Bobby. He died after being bitten by a black mamba while hunting in the Delta. Two of his forward camps were Xaxaba and Xakanaxa, now popular luxury safari lodges. The standard chalets are set in shaded surroundings and cost P850 single and P1 230 double. Bigger, more luxurious units cost P1 000 single and P1 400 double. Camping is P45 per person. They can also organise all the activities including overland camping safaris around and into the Delta. Tel 686-0222, e-mail sales@crocodilecamp. com, web www.crocodilecamp.com.

Just past the Velvet Dust Might café, is Okavango River Lodge. The crowd is younger, the chalets older and the safaris and *mokoro* trips cheaper, but similarly situated and focussed like the others. An interesting feature of this camp is that they maintain a full cricket pitch across the river on the floodplain where matches are played most Sundays. Chalets cost P220 single and P300 double, dorm beds are P90 and camping is P50 a person. Tel 686-3707, e-mail info@okavango-river-lodge.com, web www.okavango-river-lodge.com. Last up, at 19 km out of Maun, is the smart Thamalakane River Lodge (S19° 53.366, E23° 33.415). Solidly built and furnished stone and thatch bungalows, friendly staff and a large bar/lounge/dining area make this a good option along this stretch of the river. The double bungalows cost P950. Tel 686-0217, e-mail reservations@thamalakane.com, web http://thamalakane.com.

Where to eat and drink

For smart, comfortable evening drinks and dining I would suggest the Pygmy Goose restaurant at the Maun Lodge, or Harry's Bar and The Butcher's Block at Riley's Hotel. The former has pizzas and Botswanan and international cuisine, while Riley's is known for steaks, curries and fish. Both are situated on a bank of the Thamalakane River and have an upmarket atmosphere. For good all-day pub grub with a cold beer you can't beat the Buck and Hunter, opposite the airport (where the old Duck Inn used to be) or the deck in front of the Sedia Hotel out on Sir Seretse Khama Road. Both serve value-for-money pizzas, burgers, and steak and chips.

Good coffee, cake and light meals are the specialities of the restaurant on the corner opposite the airport. Alternatively, eat at the Velvet Dust Might about 15 km north of town on the road to Moremi. Although a way out of town, the Velvet Dust Might with its funky décor and interesting curios is worth the trip.

For breakfast, lunch, or just a cup of fresh coffee and a warm croissant, head for the French Connection on Mophane Avenue. Island Safari Lodge, Audi Camp, Crocodile Camp and Okavango River Lodge all serve good food and are the obvious places to eat at if you are staying there. There is one nightclub in Maun, Trekkers on Mophane Avenue, but it has a dubious reputation so go with backup. Preferably, if you are young or young-at-heart, head for The Old Bridge Backpackers. The food and drinks are basic and the people crazy, but you just might not be able to leave!

What to see and do

Scenic flights over the Delta and surrounding game areas are offered by several companies (listed below). This is the best way to appreciate how this vast aquatic system works – how the main channels, hippo paths, seasonal floodplains, lagoons and islands all integrate. A surprising number and variety of game can be spotted too. One-hour flights cost around P2500 for five passengers. This will increase as, or if, the price of fuel escalates and it obviously pays to fill the plane and bring down the individual cost. The camp you are staying at can usually book on your behalf and might help in filling the plane with other interested tourists.

Delta Air, tel 686-0044, e-mail synergy@info.bw

Mack Air, tel 686-0675, e-mail mack.air@info.bw

Northern Air, tel 686-0385, e-mail nair@kerdowney.bw

For about twice the price of a fixed-wing aircraft you can hire a helicopter. Contact **Okavango Helicopters**, tel 686-5797, e-mail okavangoheli@dyna-byte.bw or Wildlife Helicopters, tel 686-0664. All the above have offices just outside the gates of the airport.

Mokoro and power-boat trips

These trips are a fascinating and exciting way to experience the Delta up close and personal. The *mokoro* is a dug-out canoe made from a large straight tree such as a sausage or ebony tree (most are now glass fibre to save the trees) and your poler-guide will probably be a local Bayei tribesman. The first part of the trip will be a ±40-minute one by vehicle or motorboat (water levels permitting) to the poling station where the fun begins.

Your time in the Delta will be spent gliding through the channels in your

ABOVE: Water lilies attract insects and their larvae, which in turn attract birds such as jacanas.
PREVIOUS: Your *mokoro* awaits you in front of Oddballs Camp, on the Boro River in the very heart of the Okavango.

mokoro or exploring the islands on foot with your guide. You are likely to see hippos, crocs and just about any other animal that inhabits this vast wilderness. If on an overnight trip, you will camp in tents but have no amenities such as showers and toilets. Day trips cost around P600 a person (P100 single supplement), self-catered overnight trips (bring all your own food and gear) around P800 (P200 single supplement) and 2-night excursions P1000 (P300 single supplement). Fully catered overnight options, which include everything except drinks, cost about double that. All the camps listed above can organise these trips for you.

Moremi day trips

As with the *mokoro* trips, most camps in Maun can organise full-day game drives into the Moremi Wildlife Reserve. All the animals of this great game reserve can be spotted with the help of your professional guide, but it is a long way and you leave early and return late. A minimum number of 2 passengers is required at P1400 a person, although it drops to about half that if you fill the vehicle with 6 people.

Birding

Maun and the surrounding area will reward the keen birder with hours of spotting and a possible list of lifers, particularly from November to March when the summer birds are there, as well as from June or July for a month or 2 (depending on when the annual flood reaches here and how long it lasts) when the Thamalakane River is flowing. A walk along the river might produce sightings of Hartlaub's babbler, slaty egret, swamp boubou, lesser jacana, African mourning dove, pygmy goose and, if you are particularly sharp-eyed, the elusive black or Baillon's – or even a striped or spotted – crake. Birding tours of between 1 and 4 hours are offered from Afro Trek at the Sedia Hotel. Tel 686-2574.

Maun Game Reserve

This small, fenced park lies to the east of the new road bridge across the Thamalakane River and preserves the natural habitat that used to be found around Maun, before trees were chopped down in an ill-advised plan to control tsetse flies, and the town erupted economically in the 1980s and 90s. It is open daily from 07h30–18h00 and admission is free. Zebra, wildebeest and warthog are the most common species of game, but the birdlife is far more rewarding with 50 to 100 ticks possible, depending on the time of year and how sharp you are.

Other activities

Horse riding, motor boating on the Thamalakane River (water levels permitting) and cultural visits to local villages can also be arranged through your place of accommodation.

Shops and services

Medical: Maun's State Hospital is in Bringle Avenue out on the Ghanzi road, tel 686-1831 and the Delta Medical Centre is a private hospital centrally situated opposite Riley's Garage, tel 686-1411 or 686-2999, e-mail deltamed@info.bw. Okavango Pharmacy is near to the Delta Medical Centre. Dr Chris Carey operates the Medi-Help Clinic on Sir Seretse Khama Road, just past the airport turn-off (tel 686-4064) and the emergency number for Med Rescue International is 686-1831.

Motoring: Ngami Toyota is situated at the intersection of Mathiba and Tsheko-Tsheko roads (they offer a 24-hour breakdown service), tel 686-0252. Nissan is represented by Broadhurst Motors at the traffic circle at the intersection of Tsheko-Tsheko and Sekgoma roads, tel 686-4545. Lesedi Motors is the Land Rover agent and can be found down Kwena Road as you enter Maun from the Nata side, tel 686-1694. Delta 4×4 is out on the Ghanzi road and repairs and stocks spares for all 4×4 vehicles, tel/fax 686-4572.

Out on the Nata road, near to the turn-off to Lesedi Motors, is Maxi Prest Tyres for new tyres, repairs, balancing and alignment, tel 686-0588. Exact Exhausts is in the same area, tel 686-0746, while Tyre Vision fixes punctures in the main road near Ngami Toyota. Motor spares, accessories and tools are well supplied at Midas, which is in the taxi rank area, and Motovac, which is out on Mophane Avenue near to the old power station. Not all filling stations can check your tyre pressures, but Riley's always has air. Another 24-hour breakdown service is Transworld Motors, tel 686-2137.

If you need to hire a vehicle, head for the airport where Avis has offices, tel 686-0039, as well as Budget, tel 686-3728. Self Drive Adventures has a fleet of capable and well-equipped 4×4 series

70 Landcruisers for hire in Maun and are helpful with suggested itineraries. Tel 686-3755, e-mail selfdrive@ngami.net, web www.selfdriveadventures.com.

Shopping

The most central supermarket in town is the Spar, in the Ngami Centre near to the airport turn-off. This centre also houses the First National Bank, a bureau de change, Woolworths and Bateman's Fine Wine shop (which stocks the best selection of liquor in town). Across the road from the Ngami Centre is an Engen garage and another cluster of shops. Of interest here is PAAM, a shop selling hunting, camping and fishing gear, and there is also the Rendezvous Restaurant and Medi-Help Clinic.

Mathiba Road faces the airport and is home to all of the air charter companies as well as art and curio shops. The Natlee Centre, which is on the corner opposite the main airport entrance, boasts a Standard Bank with ATM, bureau de change, an internet café, travel agency, and DHL offices (tel 686-1207). Heading west on Mathiba Road will take you past the offices of Okavango Wilderness Safaris, Avis car hire and The Buck and Hunter bar. Also here you will find the Bush Boutique, which stocks a great range of camping gear, and Kalahari Kanvas, who make and repair tents and hire out equipment, tel 686-0568.

Take the first left into Mophane Avenue to find Jacana Enterprises, which sell a range of safari clothing, knives and are the local GPS fundis. Check out their wonderful website: www.jacanaent.com. Next door to them

is Motovac for spares and tools and across the road is the old power station which houses the offices of Okavango Tours and Safaris, Lodges of Botswana and The Craft Centre. The Craft Centre is a wonderful Aladdin's cave full of art, crafts and curios with an adjoining pottery and paper workshop.

Further around on your right is the water bottling plant of Aquarite where you can buy bottled water at P11 for 5 litres, or have your own tanks or bottles filled at P1.20 a litre, tel 686-0283. Even further down on the right is Trekkers nightclub – enter at your own risk! Finally, if you need washing done and the place where you are staying can't handle it (or is too expensive), try The Covenant Laundry Service on the right as you are leaving Maun on the Moremi road, tel 7160-2430, or Ever Dryclean and Laundry on the right as you leave Maun on the Ghanzi road.

Okavango Delta

The lie of the land

Starting in the highlands of Angola, around Huambo and Kuito, the Cubango River swells with summer rains and makes its way south towards Namibia. Here it forms the border as it passes Rundu and heads for the Caprivi Strip, where it swings south, cascades over the gentle Popa Falls and enters Botswana at Mohembo. Now the Okavango, the river runs dead straight for a while between 2 geological fault lines where it is called the Panhandle. This section is lined with papyrus and other water reeds that filter the water to absolute purity.

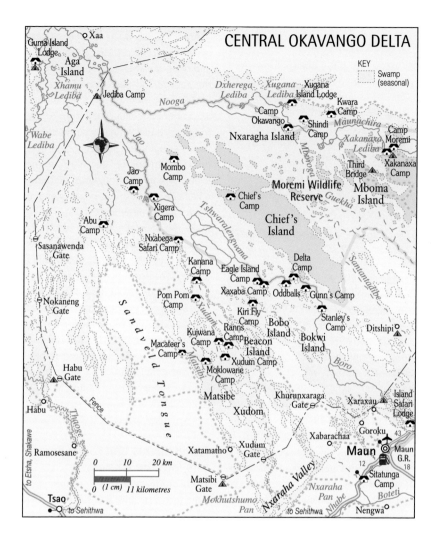

CENTRAL OKAVANGO DELTA

KEY
Swamp (seasonal)

Guma Island Lodge
Xaa
Aga Island
Xhamu Lediba
Jediba Camp
Nooga
Wabe Lediba
Jao
Dxherega Lediba
Xugana Lediba
Xugana Island Lodge
Kwara Camp
Camp Okavango
Shindi Camp
Maunachira
Camp Moremi
Nxaragha Island
Xakanaxa Lediba
Third Bridge
Xakanaxa Camp
Jao Camp
Mombo Camp
Chief's Camp
Moremi Wildlife Reserve
Mboma Island
Guekha
Xigera Camp
Tshwaralengwana
Chief's Island
Abu Camp
Nxabega Safari Camp
Sasanawenda Gate
Kanana Camp
Eagle Island Camp
Delta Camp
Santantadibe
Nokaneng Gate
Sandveld
Xudum
Pom Pom Camp
Xaxaba Camp
Oddballs
Gunn's Camp
Kiri Fly Camp
Bobo Island
Stanley's Camp
Ditshipi
Kujwana Camp
Ranns Camp
Beacon Island
Bokwi Island
Boro
Macateer's Camp
Matsib
Xudum Camp
Moklowane Camp
Habu Gate
Matsibe
Khurunxaraga Gate
Xaraxau
Island Safari Lodge
Habu
Fence
Thaoge
Xudom
Xabarachaa
Goroku
43
Ramosesane
Xatamatho
Xudum Gate
Maun
Maun G.R.
12
18
to Etsha, Shakawe
0   10   20 km
0 (1 cm) 11 kilometres
Matsibi Gate
Mokhutshumo Pan
Nxaraha Valley
Nxaraha Pan
Sitatunga Camp
Tsao
to Sehithwa
to Sehithwa
Nhbe
Boteti
Nengwa

Below the Panhandle, the river spreads and fans out into the largest inland delta in the world. From there the flood waters leave the Delta via a number of channels including Khwai to the north-east, the Thamalakane to the south-east where it passes Maun, and the Boteti to the south-west, which in times of exceptional floods reaches Lake Ngami. This magnificent, wild expanse is a mosaic of channels, lagoons, seasonally flooded grasslands and hundreds of mostly small islands – although Chief's Island accounts for a significant percentage of the entire area. For the fortunate traveller who ventures into this pristine wilderness there awaits a fantastic variety of flora and fauna – over 120 species of mammals, 440 species of birds, 70 of fishes and 60 of reptiles, not to mention the 1 300 species of plants!

This exceptional diversity of life is explained partly by the fact that the habitats in and around the Delta range from near-desert dry savanna, to seasonal wetlands, to permanent water. Also, it is a huge oasis that has been little affected by the economic activities of humankind. Game moves with the water and the seasons, as channels and lagoons fill and empty, birds come and go as conditions and migrations dictate, but always there is a seeming overabundance of life here. The big game animals include just about everything you can see in southern Africa, with particularly large numbers of elephant, lion, buffalo, leopard and hyena, giraffe, zebra and wildebeest.

Antelope are many in species and overall numbers, including the rare sable and roan. Most remarkable though are the aquatic and near-aquatic antelope of the area. Starting with waterbuck and common reedbuck that inhabit the fringes of the wet areas; you might see them several kilometres away, but they must still drink every day. Next are the lechwe, common throughout the Delta, which are always found near water and spend much of their time knee-deep in it. But most fascinating of all are the shy sitatunga, an antelope with long, splayed hooves that lurks about in the dense reed beds of the permanent wetlands, walking on the aquatic vegetation and diving into the water when alarmed or threatened. They will remain submerged, with just nostrils above water until the danger passes, and can swim significant distances like that – although they do often fall prey to crocodiles as a result. A strange and magical place indeed.

Travel agents and tour operators into the Okavango

There are more than a dozen concession areas in and around the Delta in which rights have been granted to tour operators to erect and run lodges and camps. At last count there were more than 50 of these camps and lodges, most of which cater to wealthy fly-in tourists. Rates will include all activities, sumptuous food and drinks and often your own personal guide and *mokoro* poler (those on permanent water). You will be taken on game drives or guided walks, poled to islands in the 'swamps' and generally

A lone poler drifts by on Xugana lagoon, or *lediba*, as the sun sets over the Okavango. Xugana feeds into Godikwe, which in turn feeds into Xakanaxa along sinuous hippo-patrolled channels.

made to feel like royalty in the bush. But hardly any of these operations advertise or even handle their own bookings, so it is best to contact the companies who do their promoting and marketing.

Some of the better known ones are (more or less from most to least expensive):

And Beyond Africa, tel +27-(0)11-809-4300, e-mail safaris@andbeyond.com, web www.andbeyondafrica.com

Desert and Delta, tel 686-1243, e-mail info@desertdelta.com, web www.desertdelta.com

Gunn's Camp, tel 686-0023 e-mail reservations@gunns-camp.com, web www.gunns-camp.com

Lodges of Botswana, tel 686-1154, e-mail info@lodgesofbotswana.com, web www.lodgesofbotswana.com

Moremi Safaris, tel +27-(0)11-463-3999, e-mail info@moremi-safaris.com, web www.moremi-safaris.com

Okavango Tours and Safaris, tel 686-0220, e-mail info@okavangotours.com, web www.okavangotours.com

Wilderness Safaris, tel 686-0086, e-mail okwilsaf@info.bw, web www.wilderness-safaris.com

Orient Express Safaris, tel +27-(0)21-483-1600, e-mail reservations@orient-express-safaris.com, web www.orient-express-safaris.com

For self-drive and overland travellers, the national parks booking office in Maun, tel 686-1265, fax 686-1264, is centrally situated in Kubu Street. They occupy a rather run-down pre-fab building and are open Mondays to Saturdays 07h30–12h45 and 13h45–16h30, and Sundays 07h30–12h00. Although it is notoriously difficult to get bookings in the game parks of Botswana, you stand a better chance if applying in person (see page 57 for latest booking details). You might still be told that there is nothing available, only to find the camps are sometimes empty if you just take a chance and go here. It can be frustrating to the point of infuriating, but it's just one of those things about this place that you have to learn to accept. One word of advice though, don't try this tactic of just turning up during July–August or over Easter holidays when the places are likely to be full to overflowing.

Travel agencies in Maun fall into three categories: i) the type that can book airline tickets, hotels and tours around the world; ii) those that specialise in marketing lodges and safaris in Botswana; and iii) tour operators that own and run camps and safari companies in Botswana. Of course, the functions of these different types overlap, but it's good to know the particular strengths of each.

A good example of the first kind is Travel Wild in the Natlee Centre opposite the airport gate. Able to handle any travel enquiry, they can be contacted on tel 686-0822, e-mail reservations@travelwild.co.bw, web www.travel-wildbotswana.com. An excellent and knowledgeable representative of the second variety is Okavango Tours and Safaris, which can be found in the old power station building on Mophane Avenue. Efficient, reliable and thoroughly professional, they can arrange accommodation, trips and safaris to almost any destination in Botswana. Tel 686-0220, e-mail info@okavangotours.com, web www.okavangotours.com.

Of the operators who own and run their own lodges and safari companies, Peter Sandenbergh of Lodges of Botswana probably offers some of the best choices. For those who crave decadent luxury in the middle of the Delta there is Delta Camp, complete with a comfortable and spacious tree house overlooking the water lilies and hippos. Or there is the tented accommodation of Oddballs, one of the only 'budget options' in the Delta. Both offer overnight *mokoro* camping experiences that include guided bush walks and some leisurely drifting through the channels of the Delta. Tel 686-1154, e-mail info@lodgesofbotswana.com or visit www.lodgesofbotswana.com.

Other Maun-based safari companies that can get you going are:

Bush Ways Safaris, tel 686-3685, e-mail reservations@bushways.com, web www.bushways.com

Capricorn Safaris, tel 686-1165, e-mail info@capricornsafaris.com, web www.capricornsafaris.com

But, sometimes your quickest, easiest and cheapest option is to book through the camp you are staying at in Maun – most of them run their own operations and have been doing so for many years. See under Where to stay (page 117).

Moremi and Savuti 15

If you've come to Botswana to camp in the wilderness and view game, this is most likely where you'll be heading. Not a tarred road for hundreds of kilometres, no more Spars or Woolworths and definitely no fuel from Maun all the way to Kasane: here you have to be proficient and self-sufficient. So check your gear, stock up with food and drinks, and make sure you have sufficient fuel, 'cause we're off on an adventure!

Mopane-pole bridges are a feature of Moremi. There are well-used ones at North Gate and Third Bridge and a few lesser ones in between, like this one.

Head north-east out of Maun on Sir Seretse Khama Road and, after crossing the Thamalakane River on the outskirts of town, you will reach a traffic circle. Turn left here to drive past Audi and Crocodile camps. Maybe make a quick stop at the Velvet Dust Might for ethnic clothes, innovative curios or just coffee and cake before passing the Okavango Safari Camp. Forty kilometres of tarred road ends abruptly at Shorobe village and it is another 18 km of good, wide gravel to the veterinary gate, aka 'the Buffalo Fence'. Less than 2 km further is a fork – take the left branch to Moremi's South Gate; the other way bypasses Moremi and takes you to Chobe National Park and through the sand-pit Mababe Depression.

From the fork the road starts to get a bit sandy, but it is still two-wheel-drive territory. At 3 km past the fork you will find a turn-off left to the community-run Kaziikini campsite (S19° 35.380, E23° 48.171). At P75 a person a night it is a good alternative to South Gate camp. For bookings tel +267-6800664, e-mail santawanistmt@botsnet.bw. Continue towards Moremi Wildlife Reserve and at S19° 27.568, E23° 40.389 you'll pass the turn-off left to Santawani Lodge.

Moremi Wildlife Reserve

In the early 1960s, the Batswana people were concerned about the dwindling game and rapid encroachment of cattle into their tribal hunting grounds around the eastern fringe of the Okavango Delta. With the help of conservationists and the regent, the widow of Chief Moremi III, land was set aside and in 1963 the Moremi Wildlife Reserve was proclaimed. At first it was quite small, consisting of just the Mopane Tongue – a more or less triangular piece of dry land with the points at South Gate, North Gate and Xakanaxa. In the 1970s the reserve was enlarged with the addition of the royal hunting grounds and Chief's Island (the largest tract of permanently dry land in the heart of the Delta), and in 1992 a further strip was added in the north-west, between the Jao and Nqoga channels.

The reserve can now claim to inlcude all the major Okavango habitats within its boundaries. Moremi has permanent waterways and swamplands, seasonal floodplains and two major dry areas – Chief's Island and the Mopane Tongue. With the recent re-introduction of rhino into Moremi, the reserve can now proudly claim to have the Big Five (elephant, rhino, buffalo, lion and leopard) and plenty more: hippopotamus, crocodile, cheetah, hyena, wild dog and jackal and plenty of impala, kudu, wildebeest, zebra, giraffe and warthog.

Game viewing here is always excellent and it may well have the highest all-round game densities in southern Africa. Being such a vast wetland area, it is natural that the birdlife leans toward aquatic species, many of which are migratory. Of particular interest are the lagoons where you are able to see egrets (including the rare slaty egret which in southern Africa is a near-Okavango endemic), herons and storks of many types. On top of that there are the birds of prey with at least 30 species recorded, and hundreds more. If birding is your passion, it's a case of 'see Moremi and die.'

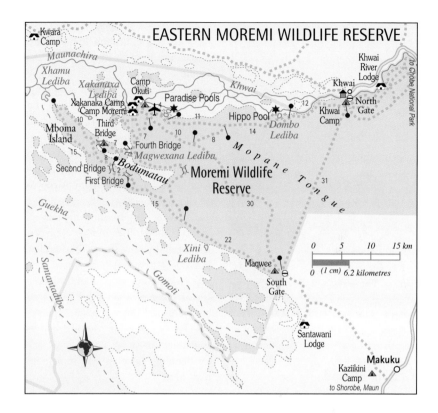

The best game-viewing months are from late April to October. These are the drier months when the grass is trampled, low and dead and surface water away from the Delta scarce, making it easy to drive around and see game. Ironically is that, from around June to September, it's also when flood water levels in the Okavango are at their highest, making it a doubly good time to be there.

It is a good idea to have a fine mesh covering your vehicle's radiator to avoid getting it blocked with dry grass and grass seeds. Also make sure the number plates are secure and out of harm's way or you'll lose them

in the deep mud wallows. Take extra care when driving through what look like small black mud puddles, or narrow water channels: they can be much deeper than you anticipate and lead to hours of recovery time and effort. Always take these crossings slowly and preferably check them out before driving through.

You will arrive from Maun at South Gate, where the opening hours from April to September are 06h00 to 18h30 and from October to March 05h30 to 19h00. Entrance fees, bookings and payments must be made in advance (see page 57) and this will be checked as you enter the reserve.

Moremi and Savuti | **133**

A marabou stork nests on a water-fig island heronry in Xakanaxa Lagoon.

Getting around

There are 3 routes beyond South (aka Maqwee) Gate: the track that bears off in a north-easterly direction follows a sandy cutline straight to North Gate; the track heading north-west goes to Xakanaxa; and the most westerly one takes you to Third Bridge. The roads in the reserve are badly signposted, so make sure you are on the right track. As most self-drivers will be heading to Third Bridge, I'll describe this route. You will need to engage 4×4 for this sandy single track that runs for 15 km through mopane forests to Xini Lagoon, a great place for spotting aquatic birds. Turning left here at the fork will take you on a loop past the lagoon, straight ahead (right) is the direct route. At 24 km from South

Gate there is a signpost (S19° 21.081, E23° 28.542) indicating left to Third Bridge and right to Bodumatau – the 'home of the lion': stay away in the wet season as it becomes a quagmire.

Keep left, and at about 38 km you will reach First Bridge. These Moremi bridges are narrow, rickety mopane-pole structures that you will have to risk when water levels are high, otherwise just drive around them. A couple of kilometres further is Second Bridge and, if you keep heading right at all forks up ahead, after another 6 km you will reach the campsite at Third Bridge. Heading left (west) here would take you on a 31 km loop around Mboma Island. It's a pleasant drive with both big trees and open grassland, generally has good game viewing and is sometimes used by a wild dog pack for denning. Cheetah also sometimes hunt here.

Third Bridge

Third Bridge has taken on mythical proportions in the folklore of the African self-drive tourist. A place to arrive at, a place to spend time at and a place to keep an eye out for lions crossing the bridge and walking through your camp at night. New ablution blocks have been constructed – hopefully the wild atmosphere that pervades this lovely spot won't be spoilt. There are only 7 sites in the camping area that are numbered and must be pre-booked (S19° 14.370, E23° 21.438). This camp has been privatised. See page 57 for details. The bridge is a long, low span through the papyrus reeds across crystal-clear water. If you are tempted to take a cooling dip to wash the dust or mud out of your hair – as many people are and do – either take extra care or preferably don't. There are crocs, and they have been known to attack!

The baboons can also be a terrible nuisance during the day, especially when you are out game driving, and love stealing anything unattended and edible. They will open storage trunks and even trailers, locked ones are tumbled until they break open, and even tents have been ripped by these thugs, so it is best to store foodstuffs in your car at all times. At night hyenas come prowling around – if the lions don't. Any food or hint of food will be a target. Even cooler boxes and leather shoes left outside tents could be dragged off and munched.

If you are spending some time at Third Bridge, there are a couple of interesting drives to do from the camp. The first is a track that starts on the eastern side of the bridge and heads off in a south-easterly direction, as if you were going to Xakanaxa. It crosses Fourth Bridge, then turns off right to continue heading south-east, heads to Bodumatau Bridge and then loops around to join the track coming up from South Gate and back to Third Bridge. This loop will be impassable in wet conditions and muddy at the best of times, so be cautious. The other is a loop that starts on the western side of the bridge and heads south-west around Mboma Island.

Xakanaxa

Most travellers aim for Xakanaxa for their next stop, which is north-east of Third Bridge. To go there cross the bridge and drive 6 kilometres to Fourth Bridge (S19° 15.130, E23° 24.130), then keep left to be heading north-east. There are various tracks as you approach Xakanaxa, which alternate between deep sand and deep channels of water. The 8 campsites are to be found past the airfield and 3 private lodges that line the river at this narrow tip of the Mopane Tongue. Elephants like to wander through the camp and the birdlife is prolific, so plan on spending a few days here too. There have been incidents of tourists being taken by crocs in the river, as well as one young camper being dragged from his open tent by lions. Do not swim in the river, and sleep in a closed tent (also for the mosquitoes).

While you're at Xakanaxa, consider taking a boat cruise through the waterways and lagoons of Moremi. Ngami Marine operates from the boat station here and offers an 8-seater boat at P430 an hour, a 12-seater at P475 and a 16-seater at P550. They also offer daily rates and self-catered or fully-catered 2- to 4-day excursions into the Delta. Tel 686-0364, e-mail nm@info.bw.

From the intersection at the airfield (S19° 11.878, E23° 25.885) you can drive south-west to South Gate. This is the 41-km direct route across the Mopane Tongue and is recommended when other routes are flooded. The more popular route is to turn off the South Gate track after 12 km (S19° 14.577, E23° 31.230) and head east parallel to the Khwai channel for another 30 km to North Gate. Note that there are many alternative bush tracks in this northern section that will become flooded in the wet season, even the main track will sometimes be blocked by deep channels or mud pits. Often there will be a wide looping track that bypasses the deepest waters and rejoins the main track further on, but exercise caution and try to travel in convoy so that help is on standby if you get stuck. The game viewing along this road is exceptional as it is also something of an animal highway all along the floodplain, pans and through the mopane forest. You should take your time along here and also consider it as a prime game-drive outing. Many visitors make a day of it.

Accommodation in Moremi Wildlife Reserve

There are 4 main campsites in Moremi: at South Gate, Third Bridge, Xakanaxa and North Gate. They have been upgraded with new ablutions, water and electricity, but I would recommend that you should still arrive completely self-sufficient and be prepared to rough it. The camps are unfenced and often invaded by all sorts of wild animals. So be extremely cautious, especially if you have young children with you. Sites at Third Bridge and Xakanaxa are limited and very popular and need to be booked in advance. Enquiries and bookings are made through various organisations (see page 57).

There are 3 lodges that can be accessed by 4×4 vehicle through the reserve (or fly-in) which are all situated at the end of the Mopane Tongue at the mouth of Xakanaxa Lagoon. The longest established lodge is Xakanaxa Camp run by Moremi Safaris. From the welcoming main building of local wood, reed and thatch overlooking the Khwai River they offer game drives, boat and *mokoro* outings. Accommodation is in en-suite luxury safari tents, which are built on platforms with views of the river and lagoon. Tariffs range from US$470 to US$875 a person a night, all inclusive, depending on the time of year. Tel +27-(0)11-463-3999, e-mail info@moremi-safaris.com, web www.moremi-safaris.com

Close by is Camp Moremi which is run by Desert and Delta Safaris. It has expansive wooden decks overlooking the lagoon, a swimming pool, elevated hide and luxury en-suite tented rooms under a riparian forest canopy. Game drives and boat trips are offered and rates are inclusive of all activities, food and drinks. Depending on the season, it will cost you between US$450 and US$850 a day to stay here. Tel +27-(0)11-706-0861, e-mail reservations@desertdelta.com, web www.desertdelta.com.

Your third option for the big splurge is the smaller and more intimate Okuti Camp operated by Ker and Downey Safaris. The main building and accommodation are clustered in traditional African-village style and have the same wonderful position and views that the other lodges have. The original rustic camp was rebuilt in 2007 to a very high standard and the accommodation is in chalets rather than luxury tents. Game drives, boat trips and all food and beverages are included: US$475–850. Tel 686-0375, e-mail safari@kerdowney.com, web www.kerdowney.com.

There are a few more lodges outside the reserve that need mentioning. The

The Mopane Tongue section of Moremi has one of the highest leopard densities in southern Africa.

Khwai River Lodge is an old established lodge just east of North Gate, which is run by Orient Express Safaris (owners of the grand Mount Nelson Hotel in Cape Town). Overlooking the vast floodplains of the Khwai River, it has all the trappings of luxury in the bush including a gym, spa and heated pool. As they are situated outside the reserve, they can offer game walks and visits to local villages as well as the normal game drives and boat trips. Accommodation in luxury en-suite tents varies between US$700 and US$1250 a person a night, depending on seasons. Tel +27-(0)21-483-1600, e-mail reservations@orient-express-safaris.com, web www.orient-express-safaris.com.

Santawani Lodge is situated just outside South Gate, 11 kilometres down a sandy track, but don't turn up unannounced – book first through e-mail info@lodgesofbotswana.com, web www.lodgesofbotswana.com. Accommodation is in solid brick and thatch en-suite chalets which cost P1850 per person, all meals and activities included.

Your final drive-in option around Moremi is the Mankwe Bush Lodge, situated east of the reserve near to Sankuyo Village on the road between Shorobe and Mababe. They offer overnight accommodation if you are just passing through or game drives and walks if you plan on staying longer. They also offer interesting packages that entail flying to Seronga from Maun, boating through the Delta and game driving back to Mankwe via Khwai River. Self-camping is available at P125 a person and en-suite tents cost P2000 if fully catered and including all activities. Tel 686-5788, e-mail mankwe@info.bw, web www.mankwe.com.

North Gate

North Gate camp (aka Khwai Camp) has many sites and is pleasantly situated under large, mature trees on the banks of the Khwai River, which teem with birds, including owls. There is a network of game tracks to the east of camp that can produce good game and bird sightings, especially if visited in the dry season. A wild dog pack often dens close to the campsite so ask if there is any action when you get there. It's also one of the best areas to see both roan and sable antelope (the other being around Santawani).

North Gate also marks the northern boundary of the Moremi Wildlife Reserve, and as you negotiate the long pole bridge across the Khwai you enter the community controlled area of raggedy Khwai village (originally founded to rehouse San-related people who lived in the Mopane Tongue area when the Moremi reserve was proclaimed). Here you will find a few little kiosks and shops selling soft drinks and canned goods. The road follows the course of the river in a north-easterly direction for about 14 km to a split in the road (S19° 06.094, E23° 49.664). Left heads off into the wilderness and eventually swings west and ends up at Seronga. This is a very difficult and obscure track and you will be told that it is on private land and off-limits. Actually it is a public road that crosses private concessions, so you can use the road as long as you do not overnight in the area between Khwai village and the vet gate near to Godigwa.

Savuti

At the previous waypoint, turn right at the split to head for Savuti and the Chobe National Park. In wet seasons you will encounter some extremely challenging water crossings and chan-

nels. If these are too deep and dangerous, head north (left) from the split for a short way and pick up a track that wanders east, then south-east and finally south, until it rejoins the road to Chobe, having avoided the worst of the flooded plains. The great thing about this area in the wet (summer) season, though, is that it attracts large flocks of water birds to the pans (particularly knob-billed and white-faced ducks) and migratory raptors like the steppe and lesser-spotted eagles that feed largely on termites.

Seven kilometres from the sign that welcomes you into Chobe National Park you will encounter another fork in the road (S19° 09.506, E23° 55.289). Right takes you south through Mababe village and on down to Maun and left to Savuti and eventually Kasane. As we want to head north, take the left fork and travel for 11 km to the official gate of the Chobe National Park. It is often unmanned, so head on through for another 21 km to yet another split in the road. Here you have the choice of keeping left for the deep sand of the Magwikhwe Sand Ridge road, or right for the (flooded in the wet) Savuti Marsh road.

They rejoin 5 km south of Savuti camp and it depends on water levels as to which one you can take. If you take this route you are likely to have to drive through plenty of very sticky black cotton mud, the kind that will entrap you at the least hesitation. The safest is left and the sand, and at S18° 45.455, E24° 00.659 you might just notice an unmarked concrete block that indicates the obscure track mentioned earlier that can lead you to Serondela and on to Shakawe. It is wise to leave early from Moremi to get to the sand ridge area (the bank of a former lake) before the day gets hot. This is when the air in the sand expands and the sand gets loose and extremely difficult to negoti-ate. Whatever time of day you tackle it, however, you should deflate your tyres to around 1 bar.

The Savuti area is so well known and popular with tourists that it is sometimes regarded as a game reserve on its own. It is, however, a section

LIVINGSTONE'S ROAD

During the mid-19th century all explorers' roads headed north through Bechuanaland. Everyone was looking for something – game, minerals, farm land or souls to save. Whatever Livingstone was looking for, his preferred route was from the mission station at Kolobeng and linked all available water sources in this generally dry, sandy country. His first watering hole was at Letlhakane, just south of present-day Orapa. From there he had the formidable Makgadik-gadi Pans to traverse, and to do this he cut through the narrow section in the middle of Ntwetwe Pan and headed for Gutsha Pan. Gutsha Pan is marked by a clus-ter of baobabs known as Green's Baobabs. Here traders, travellers and hunters used to outspan and rest and the brothers Green carved the words 'Green's Expedi-tion, 1858–1859'. Baines' Baobabs overlooking the Kudiakam Pan and near to Nxai Pan was next along the punishing route. Here it was that Thomas Baines, explorer and artist, painted this group of trees in 1862. Studying the picture today shows they have hardly changed at all over the past century and a half.

It was a long haul beyond these pans to reach the next reliable source of water, the Mababe River south of the Savuti Marsh. Today water no longer pours out of the Okavango sys-tem into the Mababe Depression and it would be a very long trek by ox wagon, around the Mag-wikwe sand ridge to the Savuti Channel. The Savuti Channel is another enigmatic watercourse, as it has filled and dried up over the years.

When Livingstone crossed it in 1851 it was a strongly flowing riv-er. But when Selous reached it in 1879, it was dry and remained so until 1957 when it started to flow again. It has since dried up again and it's anyone's guess when, if ever, it will flow again.

The shifting of tectonic plates deep underground is the reason for these changes. For travellers, the reliable Linyanti River was not far off, and then it was on to the Zambezi River, crossing at Ses-heke. Beyond the Zambezi was still terra incognito, which suited Livingstone and his fellow explor-ers just fine. So on they laboured, some never to return.

within the Chobe National Park and named after the Savuti Channel, a confusing waterway that sometimes flows from the Linyanti Swamp in the west (which forms the southern tip of the Caprivi Strip's thumb) and drains into the Mababe Depression to the south. While it is dry right now, when explorers such as Andersson, Chapman, Livingstone and Selous saw it, they recorded variously that it flowed – or not. The mysteries of the Savuti Channel and the other waterways of northern Botswana have fascinated and perplexed people for ages. Only recently has geological research confirmed the source of the mystery.

Even though we now know that tectonic burps deep underground cause the land to tilt this way and that, what no-one knows is when next it will happen, or to what effect. So it remains a mysterious process and another good reason for visiting the area. This is another place where you'll need to take precautions against grass blocking your radiator and catching alight against your exhaust pipe. There are also Bushman paintings in the hills surrounding the camp, but without a knowledgeable guide, and given the danger of leaving your vehicle, you will have difficulty finding them.

Savuti Camp (S18° 34.020, E24° 03.908) is large and there is sometimes room for an unannounced and unbooked camper. The camp is very sandy, although there is good shade, and its distinguishing feature is the ablution block built like a bomb shelter with tank-traps all around it. This is all to keep thirsty elephants from destroying the water supply (which they frequently do: it's a bit like the arms race – one side continually trying to outdo the other, with limited success). The taps that are dotted around camp are also recessed deep into concrete bollards for the same reason. There is a good network of loops and tracks around Savuti that take you into the hills or down to the Savuti Marsh, but a good sense of direction and GPS will come in handy as the tracks are poorly signposted. See page 57 for details of privitisation and bookings.

Heading out of Savuti

If you are heading from Savuti to Kasane there are 3 options. The first is a wide detour via the campsite at Linyanti. This entails 40 km of very sandy track to the north-eastern corner of the national park, on the banks of the Linyanti River. There are not many game drives in the area and the river is choked with reeds (which can be good for birding though). It's not a popular detour, but you can exit at the Linyanti Gate, head for the Ghoha Gate and then press on further north.

The most direct route to the Chobe River and Kasane is to head out of Savuti in a north-easterly direction for 28 km to the Ghoha Gate and continue through the Chobe Forest Reserve. This is a straight and very sandy track through African teak and bastard teak woodlands, which is joined by the road

The waterways of Botswana support large numbers of hippos. Around sunset males start 'yawning' — they're not tired, it's an aggressive territorial display.

A tiny painted reed frog clings to a papyrus stem in the Delta. They make a most delicate tinkling bell call.

from Linyanti at S18° 15.252, E24° 19.070. At 70 km from Savuti you will reach the village of Kachikau (S18° 09.282, E24° 29.800). If driving south from the Chobe area towards Savuti, look out for the signpost here indicating a turn-off to the left to get to Savuti. There is a general dealer here selling basics, while the road north improves with a good gravel surface. Another 40 km brings you to the big tarred road that runs between Kasane and the Namibian border at Ngoma Bridge – you might want to get down and kiss it after last seeing tar at Shorobe.

The third option from Savuti to Kasane is the pans route that loops around in a south-easterly direction from Savuti. At just over 200 km, it is slightly longer than the route through Ghoha and Ngoma gates (170 km) and it is less sandy, but it can become impassable in the wet months. Leave Savuti camp in an easterly direction heading for Quarry Hill. The road

swings south-east and after 40 km you will reach Makapa Pan. Here the road swings north for 25 km to a crossing of a water channel (S18° 33.335, E24° 27.189) and then continues for 50 km to the turn-off east to Poha Gate.

There are many pans in this area, the main one being Nogatsaa Pan at S18° 16.450, E24° 58.758. Another 60 km from the Poha Gate turn-off you will reach the main tarred road between Kasane and the Namibian border post at Ngoma Bridge. You could also exit the Chobe National Park through Poha Gate to travel 68 km to Pandamatenga on the main Nata-to-Kasane highway. But whichever route you choose, if you are driving from Maun, through Moremi, Savuti and Chobe to Kasane (including game drives), make sure you have enough food, fuel and drinking water for at least 600 km.

Accommodation in Savuti

Other than the already-mentioned campsite at Savuti, there are 2 up-market lodges in the same area. Both can be reached by 4×4 vehicle, although most visitors fly in to these lodges. Savuti Elephant Camp is run by Orient Express Safaris and offers luxury and very expensive en-suite tented accommodation overlooking the dry Savuti Channel and adjacent waterhole. Tel +27-(0)21-483-1600, e-mail reservations@orient-express-safaris.com, web www.orient-express-safaris.com.

The other is Desert and Delta's Savute Safari Lodge, on the bank of this 'stolen river'. Tel +27-(0)11-706-0861, e-mail reservations@desertdelta.com, web www.desertdelta.com.

Chobe and Kasane 16

The area around the Chobe River and Kasane in the far north-eastern part of Botswana (the Chobe District) has much in common with Namibia's Eastern Caprivi region. They are both closer to the capital cities of Zimbabwe and Zambia than their own countries' capitals.

The entrance to the Mowana Safari Lodge in Kasane ushers you into a world of safari opulence – 'lodge' being something of a misnomer.

En route

Kasane is a long way from Gaborone, which makes it less affected by Botswanan issues and more dependent on the well-being of the Victoria Falls and Zambezi tourist trade.

If you have just travelled up from Nata on the main road north you would have experienced 300 km of straight tarred road, usually potholed from the many heavy trucks that use this route and often crossed by elephant herds and other wild animals; overturned pantechnicons and animal carcasses are not uncommon sights along the way. You would have passed the turn-off to the Zimbabwean border at Pandamatenga and wondered why anyone would put an aircraft landing strip in the middle of a highway (these widened sections of road serve as emergency runways for civil and military aircraft).

Pandamatenga, or Mpandamatenga, was the old hunters' road along what is now the Botswana-Zimbabwe border. A sand track runs along the Zimbabwe side all the way to the Zambezi. The word means 'pick up and carry' for the colonial penchant for contracting 'the natives' to bear all the safari *katunda* on their heads.

Your first stop will be the border village of Kazungula. Here you can turn east for 2 km to enter Zimbabwe and travel another 73 km to Victoria Falls town, or join the queue to take the ferry straight across the mighty Zambezi to enter Zambia, then drive 60 km east to Livingstone. There is a Maxi Prest tyre service (tel 625-1033 or 7210-1525 for a 24-hr service) on your right as you enter Kazungula and then an Engen garage on your left at the turn-off to Kasane. The police station is on your right at the turn-off down to Zim and 2 km straight ahead is the border post and ferry across to Zambia.

Pray that you're not driving a truck (there were more than 120 in the queue last time I was there), and drive down to the banks of the Zambezi for the exciting trip across this great river at the junction of four countries. This is, apparently, the only place in the world where four countries – Botswana, Namibia, Zambia and Zimbabwe – share a common boundary point, and it is also the confluence of two mighty rivers, the Chobe and Zambezi. The ferry runs daily from 06h00 to 18h00.

Max Panel Beaters runs a motor vehicle workshop and breakdown service in the industrial area down the road to the Zim border (tel 625-2231 or 7167-7009) and there is a motor spares shop across the road from them. The Engen garage has a Quick Shop and takeaways. Turn off towards Kasane and after half a kilometre turn right to get to Toro Safari Lodge. An attractive pole-and-thatch complex of bar, restaurant and chalets fronts the Chobe River in pretty garden surroundings. There is a swimming pool and in the campsite each stand has its own private ablution block with hot water, power point and fireplace. They also offer fishing, boat cruises and game drives into the Chobe National Park. Standard chalets cost P573 double and camping is P75 a person. Tel 625-2694 or 7211-1283, e-mail torolodge@botsnet.bw, web www.torolodge.co.bw.

About 1 km further down the road

towards Kasane is the turn-off to the immaculate, upmarket Kubu Lodge. Luxurious thatched log cabins stand in manicured gardens overlooking the Chobe River. A well laid out nature trail winds through 30 ha of riverine forest with a great variety of birds and small animals. A sparkling pool, bar and restaurant with sundeck and a quiet, secluded campsite together with game drives and boat cruises make this the best accommodation in the area. Chalets cost P1100 single and P1400 double B&B, while camping is P100 a person. Contact Kubu Lodge on tel 625-0312, e-mail kubu@botsnet.bw, web www.kubulodge.net.

Sharon Nel from the lodge is also the driving force behind the Kazungula Children's Ark, a community-based volunteer project housed in an old school building on the property where a day-care centre is run for orphans and other needy and vulnerable children.

Next along the Kasane road is Ngina Safaris, a bit rough and tumble, but the place to visit if you are serious about fishing. The camp boasts records of a 7.8kg tiger, 3.6kg nembwe, 9.1kg barbel and 2.6kg 'pink happy'. Accommodation for 2 in an erected tent with beds costs P350 and for 4 P450. Camping is P70 a person and a limited menu is available. Tel/fax 625-0882, e-mail reservations@chobengina.com, web www.chobengina.com.

Kasane

To enter the town of Kasane turn right at the Chobe farm stall, but not before stopping there to stock up with fresh cheese, milk, yoghurt, eggs, fruit, veggies and meat. Carrying on straight allows you to bypass the town and head directly to the Chobe National Park or the Ngoma border post with Namibia. The roads around Kasane can be very potholed at times and cars swerve all over the road to avoid them, so be careful. Thebe River Safaris is the first operation you'll spy after turning down to

Elephants have made Chobe famous, but they've pummelled the riverine forest.

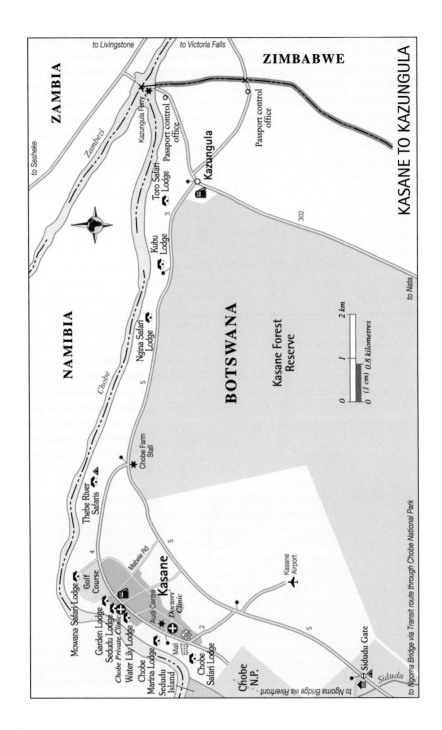

KASANE TO KAZUNGULA

to Livingstone   to Victoria Falls

ZIMBABWE

ZAMBIA

to Sesheke

Zambezi

Kazungula Ferry

Passport control office

Passport control office

Kazungula

Toro Safari Lodge

Kubu Lodge

302

to Nata

NAMIBIA

Chobe

Ngina Safari Lodge

BOTSWANA

Kasane Forest Reserve

2 km

1

0   0.8 kilometres

0 (1 cm)

0

Chobe Farm Stall

Thebe River Safaris

to Ngoma Bridge via Transit route through Chobe National Park

Mowana Safari Lodge

Golf Course

Mabele Rd

Kasane

Kasane Airport

Garden Lodge

Sedudu Lodge

Chobe Private Clinic

Water Lily Lodge

Audi Centre

Doctors' Clinic

Chobe Clinic

Sidudu Gate

Sidudu

Chobe Marina Lodge

Sedudu Island

Mall

Chobe Safari Lodge

Chobe N.P.

to Ngoma Bridge via Riverfront

Kasane. Also a bit rundown, they offer camping at P85 a person, and permanent tents for 2 at P390. They also offer game drives, boat cruises, safaris south into the Chobe National Park and day trips to Victoria Falls. Tel/fax 625-0314, e-mail thebesafaris@botsnet.bw.

Kasane town is a small, but pleasant, place with comfortable accommodation and interesting activities. It is the gateway to the northern section of the Chobe National Park and, increasingly, Victoria Falls (given Zimbabwe's prevailing political chaos). Unlike its Zambian and Zimbabwean counterpart towns, Livingstone and Victoria Falls, it is safe, laid-back and comparatively crime-free.

Activities on offer around the area are: game drives into the northern section of the Chobe National Park, boat cruises on the Chobe River for the delightful scenery, a good variety of game and birds, and day trips to the Victoria Falls. Mowana Safari Lodge is one of the smartest lodges in this part of the world and is situated on a bend in the river at the entrance to Kasane town. The impressive main building is a multistoried pole-and-thatch palace built around a huge old baobab tree. The bars and restaurants overlook the river, as do most of the rooms, and there is a riverside nature walk with a bird hide. A 9-hole golf course is available for guests and visitors to use and there are also tennis courts for hire. Single B&B rooms are P1 830 and doubles P2 690. Tel 625-0300, e-mail resmowana@cresta.co.bw, web www.crestahosp.co.za.

Continue past the golf course, which runs along the river, to the German-run Garden Lodge on your right. This comfortable home-from-home offers fully inclusive packages with accommodation, three meals and two activities a day (game drives, boat cruises, village walks or fishing) for P1 800 single and P2 750 double. Tel 625-0051, e-mail gabi@thegardenlodge.com, web www.thegardenlodge.com.

Next up along President Avenue is Sedudu Lodge, a cheaper, modest option. Also with safe off-street parking, their double rooms are in the main building and cost P400. The single rooms are located in pre-fab buildings in the garden and cost only P260. Breakfast is another P50. Tel 625-1748.

Next along the road, also on the right-hand side, is the Chobe Private Clinic for medical emergencies, tel 625-1555 or 7162-7122 (24 hrs), and next door to the clinic is the double-storied, circular design of the Water Lily Lodge. Comfortable en-suite air-conditioned twin rooms overlook the gardens and river and cost P600 a night. Their in-house Janala Tours and Safaris offers game drives, boat cruises and day trips to the Victoria Falls. Tel 625-1775, e-mail janala@botsnet.bw.

This is followed by a Spar shopping centre with a Shell garage across the road. The supermarket is well stocked and there is also a bureau de change, post office, bottle store and internet café in the complex. Opposite the Spar centre is the Chobe Photolab for all things photographic, including digital downloading. Up the hill behind them is an auto parts shop, a pharmacy, bakery for fresh, hot bread and take-aways and the Village Winery for imported liquor and speciality foods.

Croc free – the inviting swimming pool at Kubu Lodge on the banks of the Chobe.

The Department of Tourism is next along President Avenue.

This is followed by the upmarket Chobe Marina Lodge. The beautifully carved main doors of this lodge welcome you into an enormous pole-and-thatch splendour, built around a stream that runs into the Chobe River. The Riverside Bar, Commissioner's Restaurant and Mokoros Grill all nestle under mature trees and around the sparkling swimming pool. Accommodation is very comfortable and costs P2 200 single and P2 900 double, inclusive of three meals and two game activities a day. African Odyssey is on site to offer game drives and river cruises, while conference facilities are also available. Tel 625-2221, e-mail res1@chobemarinalodge.com, web www.chobemarinalodge.com.

Across the road from the Chobe Marina Lodge is the Audi Centre, a small but important cluster of shops. There is a stationery shop, art gallery, computer outlet for internet, fax and international phone calls, Kingfisher Trading, which stocks fishing and camping gear, maps, clothing, knives and binoculars and the Gallery Africa for curios, coffee and cakes.

Next door is another medical doctor at the Chobe Medical Centre, tel 7160-4264, and the Kasane Primary Hospital is also near here, tel 625-0333. The police station is next on your left and then the turn-off up left to join the A33 main road to the Namibian border at Ngoma Gate. Opposite the turn-off is another shopping centre, this one housing Choppies supermarket, an FNB ATM, bureau de change, bottle store and internet service.

To continue on President Avenue, past the turn-off, would bring you to the Chobe Safari Lodge, yet another impressive pole-and-thatch structure recently rebuilt on multiple levels down to a jetty on the river. This is the oldest inn in Kasane with a history that stretches back to the pioneering days. New riverfront rooms, a squash court, a very well-stocked curio shop with clothes, books and maps and a stream running through it all, make this lodge a perennial favourite with travellers. Room rates are P890 double and, importantly, they offer a nice centrally situated campsite at P65 a person. Tel 625-0336, e-mail reservations@chobelodge.co.bw, web www.chobesafarilodge.com.

Other information

Buses and minibuses leave for Nata from behind the Shell garage in the centre of town. Avis car hire operates from the Mowana Safari Lodge as well as the local airport, tel 625-0144. Air Botswana flies between Gabarone and Kasane 3 times a week, Sundays, Tuesdays and Fridays, tel 625-0161. The airport is just out of town, off the A33, which heads towards Ngoma Bridge. Chobe Nissan (tel 625-0673) and Zambezi Toyota (tel 625-0747) will fix most vehicles, and

DHL couriers is near to Kubu Lodge in Kazungula, tel 625-0069.

Chobe

Now that you have rested, relaxed and stocked up in Kasane, let's head west to enter the riverfront section of the Chobe National Park. Separated from the rest of the national park by the A33 main road west to Ngoma Gate border post, the riverfront section and its animals enjoy year-round easy access to water under a canopy

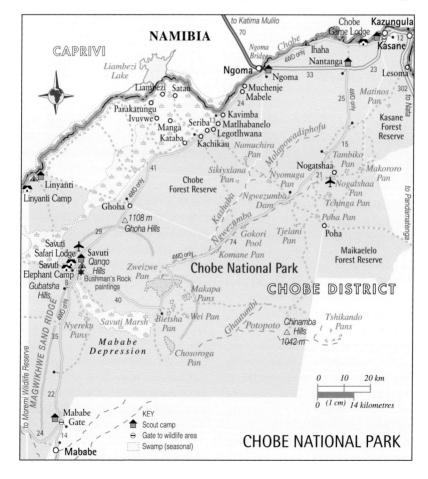

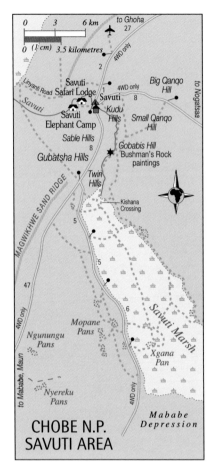

The main entrance into the park from Kasane is Siduku Gate (S17° 50.595, E25° 08.615). Here your bookings will be checked before you meander down the track towards the river. Head in a westerly direction to pass the Chobe Game Lodge, making use of the loop road options that take you down onto the floodplain. Some tracks can be very sandy and others, like on the Puku Flats, are flooded in the wet season. Distances are short, so drive slowly and you will reach the old abandoned campsite of Serondela at 16 km from the gate. This park has possibly the best representation of antelope in southern Africa, with sable, roan, tsessebe, oribi, impala, wildebeest, eland, kudu, waterbuck, reedbuck and lechwe, which are confined to floodplains. The specials of this area are the Chobe bushbuck, which has darker markings than the bushbuck elsewhere, and puku, which stick to the most rank areas of the floodplain. A good number of predator sightings can also be expected.

It is only another 15 km (or more, depending on your detours) to reach Ihaha campsite (S17° 50.478, E24° 52.748). Its beautiful position on the edge of the Chobe River makes up for the poor condition of the ablution block. Close encounters with monkeys, baboons and elephants explain the state of the amenities here. Just remember, at all times, there are many, very big crocs in the river, which sometimes come out the river at night to take a look around (never sleep out in the open, or in an unclosed tent).

Many visitors to this part of the park will probably stay at a lodge in

of mature leafy riparian forest. Large herds of buffaloes, prides of lions and the highest concentration of elephants in Africa can be found along the banks of the Chobe River. The truth is, it used to be a lot leafier here, as the elephants have had a massive impact on the riverine vegetation. Birdlife is varied and plentiful too, with kingfishers, bee-eaters, fish eagles, cormorants, herons, egrets and plovers being just some of the common varieties.

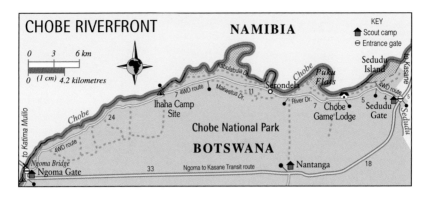

CHOBE RIVERFRONT

NAMIBIA

KEY
🏠 Scout camp
⊖ Entrance gate

0   3   6 km

0 (1 cm) 4.2 kilometres

Sedudu Island

Chobe National Park

BOTSWANA

Ngoma Bridge
Ngoma Gate   33   Ngoma to Kasane Transit route   Nantanga   18

Ihaha Camp Site

Chobe Game Lodge

Sedudu Gate

to Katima Mulilo

Kasane and drive into the park for the day. However, nothing beats the excitement of staying in the park and hearing the sounds of the bush at night, or the adrenaline rush of facing an elephant on your way to the camp's ablution block.

You have two accommodation options along this riverfront section: basic camping or five-star luxury. The Chobe Game Lodge is very much in the film-star league and has every luxury you would expect from a place that quotes in US$. Its heydays were when Liz Taylor and Richard Burton (the actor, not the explorer) honeymooned here (their second marriage). All activities, food and drinks are included, and visits to this lodge are often combined with other lodges and camps in the Desert and Delta Safaris portfolio. For special packages contact Desert and Delta on tel +27-(0)11-706-0861, e-mail reservations@desertdelta.com, web www.desertdelta.com. Fortunately, for those with simpler tastes and budgets, the park offers camping at the Ihaha campsite (see page 57 for details).

West of Ihaha you have the option of heading inland, away from the river to do some bush game-viewing. But eventually you will reach the Ngoma Gate where you join the A33 again. From here you can continue west and cross into Namibia over the Ngoma Bridge, east will take you back to Kasane, or cross over the A33 and head south down to Savuti and Maun.

The tiger's fearful symmetry of teeth and sleek fighting lines makes it the favoured sporting catch in Africa.

NW – Shakawe, Panhandle, Tsodilo, Drotsky's 17

If you have become blasé about Botswana's more popular sights, tired of making way for safari wagons carrying cosily wrapped and pampered clients, then the north-west is your new frontier. It's how old-timers remember Botswana used to be – inexpensive, wild and rough. They still welcome the self-driver and you will need all the off-road paraphernalia you have been longing to use. And why's it called a 'panhandle'? Any map will show that the Okavango Delta is more or less circular – like a pan – and the Okavango River between Shakawe and Seronga runs pan-handle straight between two parallel geological faults.

LEFT AND ABOVE: This beautiful San painting of rhinos is just one of thousands to be found in the Tsodilo Hills. The cliffs rise up impressively from the featureless surrounding sand plains.

The lie of the land

The small size and lack of amenities at Shakawe is indicative of how isolated and undeveloped the Panhandle area is. This town has only recently acquired a basic supermarket and a fuel station, but both still sometimes run out of supplies – much like Maun of the 1970s.

The easy way to reach Shakawe is up the tarred road from Sehithwa, which in turn is linked to Ghanzi and Maun by good roads. For about 300 km north from Sehithwa, the road skirts the western edges of the Delta to Seronga. Then it follows the Okavango River all the way up past Shakawe to the Namibian border at Mohembo.

This opens another way into the Panhandle region, via Namibia. Access from Namibia's Caprivi Strip is on tarred roads to the bridge across the Kavango River at Bagani, where fuel supplies are erratic. From there you go south for 30 km on good gravel past Popa Falls and through the Mahango Game Park. Park entry fees are not payable if you are just passing through on your way to the Botswanan border, but note that you are not allowed to travel through the park on a motorcycle, making this route impassable for bikes. For four-wheelers, however, this offers you the options of coming across from Etosha National Park and Bushmanland in the west, or from Katima Mulilo in the east. By using the Mohembo border you can also plan a round trip north from Maun via Moremi, Savuti, Kasane and then west into Namibia's Caprivi to re-enter Botswana at Shakawe.

Although other guidebooks discour-age it and even say it can't be done, there is one other way to approach the Panhandle, and that is from the Moremi/Savuti area in the east. The track in question heads north and then west from just outside the Moremi game park. Leave the reserve across the bridge at North Gate and travel north-east along the Khwai River for about 11 km. At S19° 06.094, E23° 49.664 there is a fork – the main road swings right to Mababe village and on up to Savuti, but the left fork will eventually get you to Betsha on the northern edge of the Delta.

This is an indistinct track with no villages or support along the way. You will probably not see another vehicle and if you do break down, you will have to save yourself. From Betsha the track improves to Seronga and then there is a decent gravel road up to the Mohembo ferry (S18° 16.602, E21° 47.260) where you can cross the Okavango River. This ferry runs between 06h00 and 18h30 and is free. From the western bank of the river it is 2 km north to the Namibian border and 10 km south to Shakawe. This route travels through concession areas north of the Delta – so again you will be very unwelcome and not be allowed to overnight along the way. Have I made it sound attractive enough? In truth it is a potentially hazardous, difficult route and I shouldn't even be suggesting it, but hey, this is Africa!

Shakawe and surrounds

It is now possible to buy most basic foodstuff and even fuel in Shakawe. The Shell pumps, Choppies supermarket and Barclays Bank are clustered around the turn-off to Mohembo while

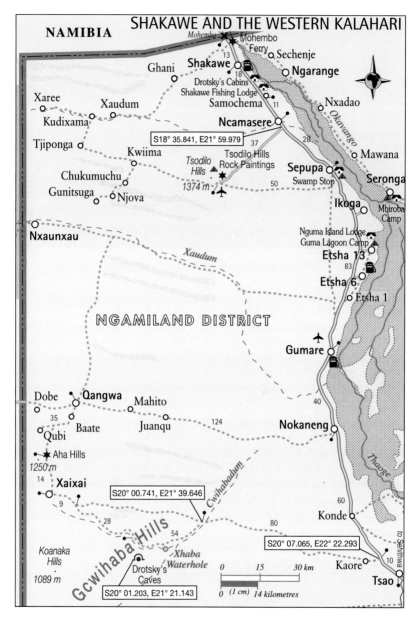

SHAKAWE AND THE WESTERN KALAHARI

NAMIBIA

Mohembo
Mohembo Ferry
Sechenje
Ghani
Shakawe 13
Ngarange
18
Drotsky's Cabins
Shakawe Fishing Lodge
Xaree
Xaudum
Samochema 11
Nxadao
Kudixama
Ncamasere
S18° 35.841, E21° 59.979 37
28
Tjiponga
Kwiima
Tsodilo Hills Rock Paintings
Sepupa
Mawana
Chukumuchu
Tsodilo Hills
Swamp Stop 50
Seronga
Gunitsuga
Njova
1374 m
Ikoga
Mbiroba Camp
Nxaunxau
Nguma Island Lodge
Guma Lagoon Camp
Xaudum
Etsha 13
83
Etsha 6
Etsha 1
NGAMILAND DISTRICT
Gumare
Dobe
Qangwa
Mahito
40
35
Juanqu
124
Qubi
Baate
Nokaneng
Aha Hills
1250 m
14
Xaixai
S20° 00.741, E21° 39.646
9
Konde
28
54
80
S20° 07.065, E22° 22.293
60
Koanaka Hills
Xhaba Waterhole
Kaore
10
Gcwihaba Hills
Drotsky's Caves
0   15   30 km
Tsao
1089 m
S20° 01.203, E21° 21.143
0 (1 cm) 14 kilometres

Okavango

Cwihabadum

Thaoge

to Sehithwa

Shakawe village is 1 or 2 km further north. There you'll find a general dealer, auto parts shop, butcher and bottle store (where the intercity bus also conven-iently stops). Shakawe clinic is on the right-hand side of the main road and a doctor has a practice on the left just past the shops.

The Mohembo ferry crosses the Okavango River north of Shakawe and the Panhandle region, and just south of the Caprivi Strip — deep in old Africa.

There is no tourist accommodation in Shakawe village, but about 7 km south of town is the first of 3 satellite lodges. At S18° 25.578, E21° 51.974 is a rusty old sign depicting a Cape clawless otter at the turn-off east to Drotsky's Cabins. A short drive down a leafy lane brings you to this old, established camp, sitting on a high bank overlooking the swift-flowing, mighty Okavango. A rustic restaurant and bar is built out on stilts over the river, huge trees line the banks and lush gardens surround it. Accommodation is in A-frame bungalows of different sizes that sleep up to 5 people. The campsite is densely wooded with good ablutions, but a thick reed bed hides the river. The river and reed beds are already quite wide here and fishing and birding are the main activities. Fishermen hope for bream (tilapia) and tiger fish, while birders pray for a glimpse of the elusive Pel's fishing owl or African skimmers – boats and

tackle are for hire. A-frame accommodation is P750 single, P1 020 double and P1 215 a night for the unit that sleeps 5. Camping costs P155 a person a night and includes firewood and plug points. Tel 687-5035, e-mail drotskys@info.bw, web www.drotskycabins.com.

The Drotskys, one of the area's pioneering white settler families, also run a more exclusive and difficult-to-reach operation, Xaro Lodge. Set on an island about 8 km downstream from Drotsky's, it is accessible only by boat. Gardens and large established trees complement the solid stone and thatch main building while accommodation is in permanent en-suite tents set on wooden decks. They cost P1 000 single a night and P1 540 double. Activities and contact details are the same as for Drotsky's Cabins.

About 4 km south of Drotsky's turn-off is the road down to the Shakawe Fishing Lodge (S18° 26.794, E21°

53.653). Another 2 km through a small village brings you to this very friendly and homely operation. The river bank is more open here and all accommodation overlooks lily-filled channels. Ten spacious, but basic, units offer en-suite accommodation with braai areas outside, while the campsite is clear and open with good access to the river. Guided boat trips for fishing or birding are offered and there is usually a good chance of seeing Pel's fishing owl. Book through Travel Wild in Maun, tel 686-0802, e-mail safaris@travelwild.co.bw, web www.travelwildbotswana.com.

Between Drotsky's and Shakawe Fishing Lodge is a turn-off marked by two large crocodile statues. From here it is 1.6 km down to the Krokovango Crocodile Farm where they do research and breeding. They also offer guided tours and are open Mondays to Saturdays from 08h00 to 17h00. The best time to visit is at feeding times which are Tuesdays and Saturdays at 11h00.

But before we leave the bright lights of Shakawe there is another accommodation option that beats all the rest, Okavango House Boats. They operate 3 houseboats: the *Ngwesi* (accommodates 8 people), *Inkwazi* (15 people) and *Inyankuni* (max 24 people) which all operate on the Okavango's main stream between Sepopo and Seronga. With a friendly and knowledgeable crew of 2, the boat is at your command to chug off into the channels and floodplains to fish, view game and birds or just relax and enjoy the idyllic surroundings. The food is delicious (lots of fish), the drinks are cold and there is a small motorboat tender to take you on excursions. This is probably the best way to experience the Okavango in a relaxed and comfortable way. It costs P5 000, plus fuel, to hire each boat for a day. The price includes the crew, tender and tackle. An extra P360 a day a person buys you 3 meals, but drinks cost extra. Tel 686-0802, e-mail krause@info.bw, web www.okavangohouseboats.com.

Tsodilo Hills

At 32 km south of Shakawe is the turn-off west (S18° 35.841, E21° 59.979) to Botswana's most important historical site, Tsodilo Hills. A much-improved road (the 35 km will take you about 35 mins) brings you to a small village where you must turn right to enter the gates of this World Heritage Site. Rising from the sandy surroundings are four massive granite hills, known as the Male, Female, Child and Grandchild. The peak of the largest inselberg is, at 1 395 m above sea level, the highest point in Botswana. But it is the rock art that the whole area is famous for; with some 4 000 images at 400 sites confined to 10 sq km, it is one of the highest concentrations of rock paintings in the world.

The red ochre that has been used to paint scenes of animals, humans or abstract designs occurs naturally in Tsodilo's rocks. Blood, plant sap and heated fat were probably used as fixatives. Paintings were executed by the San people, for whom the granite hills were a sacred place, and whose descendants still live in the area. Legend has it that Tsodilo is the birthplace of humankind: we certainly now know from DNA research that the San's is

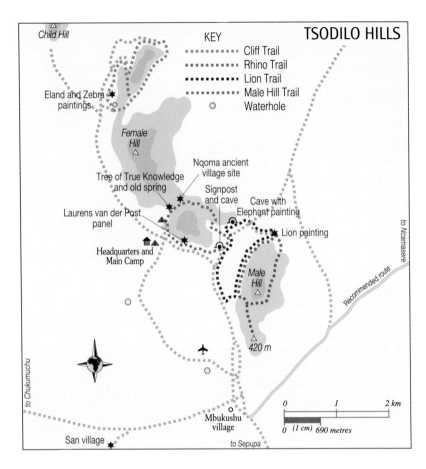

KEY

.... Cliff Trail
.... Rhino Trail
■■■■■■■■■■ Lion Trail
.... Male Hill Trail
○　　Waterhole

TSODILO HILLS

Child Hill

Eland and Zebra
paintings

Female
Hill

Tree of True Knowledge
and old spring

Nqoma ancient
village site

Signpost
and cave

Cave with
Elephant painting

Laurens van der Post
panel

Lion painting

Headquarters and
Main Camp

Male
Hill

to Ncamasere

Recommended route

420 m

to Chukumuchu

0   1   2 km

0   (1 cm)   690 metres

Mbukushu
village

San village

to Sepupa

the oldest human lineage on earth.

Painting was done using a finger or frayed stick ends – although in places such as the Drakensberg animal hair brushes were known – and most date from between 800 and 1200 AD. A few distinctive white paintings have been made using the locally abundant white chalk-like calcrete. First recorded on a map by John Arrowsmith in 1857, it was the German explorer Siegfried Passarge who sketched many of the paintings in 1898. But it was Laurens van der Post's book *The Lost World of*

the Kalahari that brought the hills and their paintings to the attention of the wider world in 1955.

To get the best out of your visit to the hills you will need to hire a local guide. He will locate some of the hidden paintings and explain some interesting folklore along the way. The main walking trail to reach the best sites is the Rhino Trail on the Female Hill, which starts close to the offices and campsite. It starts with panel 1 depicting rhino, eland and possibly a donkey; panel 2 shows a wagon wheel and donkeys that could be evidence of contact with Europeans; panel 3 is a rock face with eland, kudu, spider and springhare; 4 is the famous so-called Van der Post panel depicting mainly giraffe and eland; around a corner is a cave shelter 5, and then 6 is a painting with what looks like a whale (although it could more likely be a mythical rain creature) and a penguin. The San were highly mobile, and these images could have been seen, or passed on through oral means, from the Namibian coastline. Panel 10 contains the most striking paintings of rhinos; 11 has men dancing with erect penises, something that is a fairly common characteristic of San rock paintings elsewhere.

There are thousands more paintings, none of which were marked when we were there, which again is good reason to hire a guide so you can get the most out of your visit. Official guides can be found at the information centre and museum that has been built near to the public campsite. The museum has baskets, jewellery, bags and pots on display and highlights not just the San involvement in Tsodilo, but the later arrival of Bantu tribes as well.

The public campsite is rather basic, but has a good ablution block. There is no other accommodation, shops or fuel available in the area, so you will have to be completely self-sufficient for the duration of your stay. The nearby village is disappointingly devoid of any Bushmen, but if you are looking for something other than paintings to photograph, head north-west away from the camp at sunset for the most beautiful shots of the hills glowing red as the sun drops. Tsodilo is managed by the Department of National Museums and the local community, and there seems to be some confusion as to who runs what and how much to charge. On our visit we were charged no entrance or camping fees and paid only P70 for our guide. Check with: e-mail nationalmuseum.gov.bw, web www.mysc.gov.bw/nmmag.

Sepupa and Seronga

Back on the main road south it is 25 km from the Tsodilo Hills intersection down to Sepupa. There is a signposted turn-off down a tarred road to this little village that has a general dealer, but no fuel. Halfway down this road, before reaching the village there is a turn-off right to The Swamp Stop (S18° 44.754, E22° 11.807). With 7 new en-suite cha-lets to augment their permanent tents and campsite, they also offer boat trans-fers across the Panhandle to Seronga (for *mokoro* trips), fishing, birding and a launching ramp if you have brought your own boat. Camping costs P85 a person, serviced tents P320 (sleep 2) and double chalets P640. Tel 686-4636, e-mail res@swampstop.co.bw.

The 90-minute Seronga transfers will cost you P1500 for a small boat and P1800 for a large boat, one way. You can also drive to Seronga from Shakawe by taking the Mohembo ferry (see page 154) across the Okavango River and taking a fairly good gravel road down the eastern side of the Panhandle. Two

The comfortable *Ngwesi* houseboat offers air-conditioned cabins and raised viewing deck. It will moor anywhere you fancy along the Panhandle.

kilometres south of Seronga is Mbiroba Camp run by the Okavango Polers Trust. This trust was established in 1998 by polers from the local community who wanted to offer affordable access to the Delta and profit directly from their endeavours. It has been a notable success and offers travellers the chance to experience true Bayei and Hambukushu culture while staying at the Mbiroba Camp.

Of course, the affordable *mokoro* camping trips are the real reason for visiting and you can tailor any length of trip, including guided walks on the islands. Mbiroba Camp accommodation in rondavels costs P385 a person. Camping at shaded sites on the floodplain is P75 a person. *Mokoro* trips are all self-catering (bring your own food and camping gear) and cost P1 650 per *mokoro* per day. Contact them on tel 687-6861, e-mail polers @okavangodelta.co.bw, web www. okavangodelta.co.bw.

There is a signposted turn-off (S18° 59.121, E22° 17.332) 43 kilometres south of Sepupa, going east to Nguma Island Lodge. A sandy 4×4 track winds for 12 km down to this solidly built and maintained lodge on the edge of the Nguma lagoon. The fishing and birding are good and boats and *mekoro* are for hire. Raised wooden walkways connect the luxury en-suite tents to the large bar/ restaurant area while the comfortable, shaded campsite, called Delta Dawn, is kept well separate. Lodge rates of P1 520 a person sharing include accommodation, meals and activities such as boat and *mokoro* trips, use of fishing tackle, guided walks and laundry.

Camping is P105 a person and there are twin-bedded units on stilts in the Delta Dawn campsite at P750 a night. Rules and regulations are strictly enforced so check them out; tel 687-4022, e-mail gumacamp@dynabyte.bw, web www. ngumalodge.com.

There is another, much more casual camp nearby called the Guma Lagoon Camp, which is popular with fishermen. Catering mainly for the self-driver, there is a large, equipped kitchen for all to use as well as fridge and freezer facilities. Situated just south of Nguma Island Lodge, the access road is through the village of Etsha 13 and on for another 13 km of sandy 4×4 track. Three erected tents, each with their own beds, linen and private bathroom, are P575 a night (double) and camping in your own tent costs P90. Tel 687-4626, e-mail info@guma-lagoon.com, web www.guma-lagoon.com. Both the

Exiting the inky darkness of Drotsky's Caves into the bright light of the Gcwihaba Hills. The roots of a rock fig seem to make the dolomite walls an eerie, living thing.

above-mentioned establishments can arrange transfers if you cannot reach them with your own vehicle.

Routes to Drotsky's Caves

Etsha 6 is a short way off the main road south of Guma Lagoon and does boast a bottle store, a poorly stocked supermarket and petrol pumps that

– usually – have fuel. However, you are far better off heading on another 33 km to Gumare where there are two garages, an Engen and a Shell, opposite each other. The Shell station has a well-stocked convenience store with ice, an FNB ATM and also sells take-aways. A run into town will bring you to a small shopping centre

is a turn-off (S19° 39.575, E22° 10.995) west signposted to 'Qangwa – 120'. This indicates 120 km of bad road to Qangwa (S19° 31.852, E21° 10.270) far out in the wild west of the Kalahari. There is nothing much to see or do out there, just a few scattered Bushman villages, so be well provisioned and prepared. It is, however, an adventurous route in or out of the country as the track continues west of Qangwa (there are different spellings) for another 20-odd km to a forlorn and forgotten border post with Namibia; but it is official and operational. Another 57 km of sandy tracks on the Namibian side will bring you to Tsumkwe, from where it is 185 km on a gravel road to join the B8 route to Grootfontein. Or you could swing south from Qangwa to travel through the villages of Dobe and XaiXai, then east to eventually reach Drotsky's Caves. Whichever route you take in this far western Kalahari wilderness, you must realise how easy it is to get into serious difficulties if you are not properly equipped and driving a tough, reliable 4×4 vehicle.

A more direct route to Drotsky's Caves (aka Gcwihaba Caverns) is to turn west 10 km north of the village of Tsao. Signposted to Gcwihaba at S20° 07.065, E22° 22.293, the gravel road starts out well enough with patches of sand alternating with wallows that would be muddy in the wet. After 8 km you will pass a school and a few huts and at 41 km you pass through a vet fence. The cleared section of road ends at 77 km and the track becomes narrow and winding. At

where there is a Barclays Bank, bottle store, pharmacy and the basic-looking Joretti Medical Centre (tel 687-4886 or 7181-9073). The government hospital is further into town and C Tree Panel Beaters offers a 24-hr breakdown service as well as all mechanical repairs (tel 7278-4875 or 7162-7711).

Continuing south down the main road towards Sehithwa, you'll reach the village of Nokaneng where there

80 km (S20° 00.741, E21° 39.646) the road forks and there is an old wooden sign indicating Gcwihaba to the left. Keep left here, since right would take you on the northern route directly to XaiXai. You will reach the deserted cattle post of Xhaba at 97 km, where you must keep left to pass through it. The track becomes very sandy now as you cross vegetated dunes and the bushes scratch your vehicle's paintwork. At around 122 km you must ignore the tracks leading off to the right and keep left up a valley with low cliffs on each side. A few kilometres further (S20° 01.203, E21° 21.143) keep left again and climb a very sandy hill to reach the entrance to the main caves.

Drotsky's Caves

The caves were first brought to the attention of the outside world when local Bushmen showed Ghanzi farmer Martinus Drotsky the caves in 1932. The surrounding hills and caverns were declared a national monument in 1934, but since then not much exploration has been done. It has been established that the area has been occupied for at least 12 000 years, as some ancient charcoal, bones and ostrich eggs have been found in the caves – but no rock art. There are some archaeological excavations now underway.

Don't expect entrance gates, neat steps with handrails and well-lit halls – you will need your own strong torch, good walking shoes and, until recently, a big ball of string to find your way out again. Amenities are being built, and guides appointed by the national museum can show you around, but you'll still need your ball of string if you want to venture in one end and out the other. The main entrance is down into a great hole in the side of a hill. The roots of strangler figs follow you down as you are swallowed up into the darkness that hides beautiful formations of stalactites (hang down) and stalagmites (grow up).

Formed in rare dolomitic marble (metamorphosed limestone) over millions of years, acidic water has eroded the alkaline calcareous rock to form the caverns. Bats are the most numerous inhabitants of the caves, along with spiders and cockroaches, but the caves are also supposed to harbour porcupines and even an occasional leopard! Switch your torches off to get an idea of how dark darkness can really be, but don't go stumbling around in the dark – there is a deep pit forming an obstacle around the middle of the system. If you can negotiate this, then the northern exit is not far. But remember, a GPS will not work in here!

Camping is allowed at designated areas around the caves, but there are no amenities. Entrance to the area is P50 a person, a guide will cost a minimum of P20 a person, and camping is another P20. But, if there are no officials around at the time there is no charge. For more info, contact the National Museum at e-mail nationalmuseum@gov.bw, web www.mysc.gov.bw/nmmag.

To return to the main Sehithwa-Shakawe road you can return the way you came back to Tsao, or loop around via XaiXai and Qangwa to Nokaneng. You might even be adventurous enough to try the route across the border to Tsumkwe in Namibia.

Ghanzi and the Central Kalahari

18

Ghanzi is only 300 kilometres from Maun, but what a difference – you could be in another country!

A San elder teaches youngsters about *veldkos* in the Central Kalahari. They might well be the last generation of the world's 'first people' to experience things as they were in the beginning.

Ghanzi

Ghanzi is a working town serving a relatively wealthy ranching community. Its roots are not hunters and adventurers, but rather struggling stock farmers who had to come to terms with the harsh environment and local San people who considered it their hunting ground. Now the San too are having to adapt and fight for their rights and land. But, it's a wonderful place where the *boere* speak *boesmantaal* and the *boesmans* speak *boeretaal*.

For anyone who had the good fortune to visit Ghanzi in the 80s or before, it will come as a shock to see the town now. Back then, if the Hollandia Store didn't stock it, you went without, and the lone petrol pump out front was hand operated. The Kalahari Arms was a Wild West saloon filled with farmers drinking 'spook and diesel' (brandy and Coke), while outside the bottle store lay locals passed out drunk in the sun. Now it's all gentrified with tarred roads laid out in a grid pattern, shopping malls, a Shell garage with a convenience store, and the Kalahari Arms has DStv and – can you believe – a conference centre!

We have the Trans-Kalahari Highway to thank (or blame) for this, as it now takes hours instead of days to reach Ghanzi from Namibia in the west, or Lobatse in the south. And with only 300 km of excellent tarred road to Maun, Ghanzi has become very much a part of the tourist circuit. Easy access to the vast wilderness of the Central Kalahari Game Reserve and even the Kgalagadi Transfrontier Park in the south is drawing more travellers to this friendly little town in the middle of nowhere.

Coming from the north or south, your point of entry into Ghanzi is to turn off at the Shell garage, which stands opposite the tourism bureau.

Mrs Nelie de Graaff – of pioneer Lemcke-Lewis stock – presides over the Hollandia Store in Ghanzi.

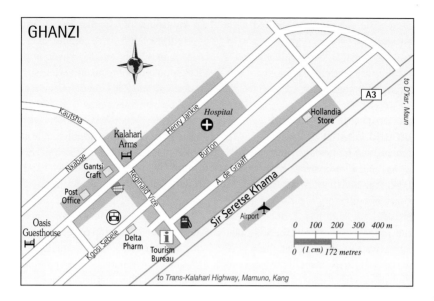

GHANZI

to D'kar, Maun

A3

Kautsha

Hollandia
Store

Hospital

Henry Jankie

Kalahari
Arms

Burton

Nxabae

A. de Graaff

Gantsi
Craft

Reginald Vize

Sir Seretse Khama

Post
Office

Oasis
Guesthouse

Koosi Sebele

Airport

0   100   200   300   400 m

Delta
Pharm

i

Tourism
Bureau

0   (1 cm) 172 metres

to Trans-Kalahari Highway, Mamuno, Kang

The little-used Ghanzi airport is across the road. You will probably need to refuel at the garage and you can pump tyres there and shop at their convenience store too. The road into Ghanzi runs straight into the Kalahari Arms Hotel, passing along the way a tyre service on the right and spares shop on the left.

There is a small shopping centre at the Kalahari Arms T-junction which contains a Choppies supermarket and, if you turn left here into Henry Jankie Avenue, you will find another small shopping centre with a well-stocked Spar supermarket and Barclays Bank. Across the road from Spar is the excellent and authentic Gantsi Craft, while down a side street behind them is Artok Butchery for vacuum-packed meat and biltong. There is a bottle store and take-aways in the Kalahari Arms. If you turned right at this T-junction (again into Henry Jankie Avenue) you

would find Koko's Tasty Chicken take-aways and, further down, the state hospital on your right.

To experience living history and chat to one of the area's most interesting and knowledgeable characters, turn right directly after the Shell garage into De Graaff Road and stop in at the Hollandia Store. In her 80s now, Mrs Nelie de Graaff grew up in Ghanzi as Miss Lemcke. Her mother was a Lewis of pioneer stock who at 16 gave birth to her and went on to pass away at the ripe old age of 97. Nelie married Mr de Graaff from Holland (hence the shop's name) and started the De Graaff dynasty which now owns large farms in the area. Her son, Christiaan, has been appointed Minister of Agriculture in the Ian Khama government and other son Willie runs the wonderful game farm Grasslands. It's amazing what you can learn over an ice-cold Coke on a quiet day in timeless Hollandia

Store! The store is still stocked with an amazing variety of goods – pop in and support this lovely old lady, you'll come away with far more than just what you bought.

Accommodation in and around Ghanzi

I'm a sucker for nostalgia and although it has been extensively modernised, I like the Kalahari Arms. The bar is smart and comfortable, the restaurant is well run and has a good menu, the rondavel accommodation is quiet and private, there is a swimming pool and the staff are friendly. What more do you want? There's even camping available. Single rooms are P400, double rondavels P460 and 2-bedroomed units that sleep 4 cost P590 a night. The small campsite is grassed with neat ablutions and costs only P30 a person. Contact them on tel 659-6298, e-mail kalahariarmshotel@botsnet.bw, web www.kalahariarmshotel.com.

Your alternative accommodation in town is the Oasis Guest House, which is upstairs in the Green Centre on the western end of Henry Jankie Avenue. Each room has tea- and coffee-making facilities, but shares ablutions. There is no bar or restaurant, but rates are a reasonable P220 single and P320 double. Tel/fax 659-7853.

There are 3 camps and lodges south of Ghanzi, the best being Thakadu Camp which is managed and hosted by the owners Jeanette and Chris Woolcott. Thakadu is situated on a game farm and the main dining area overlooks a natural pan. Known for its cosy bar and excellent food, it is 4.5 km south of Ghanzi, and 3 km east of the main road. Accommodation is in domed tents at P165 single and P220 double, or more luxurious tents at P345 single and P465 double. Camping with your own equipment is P50 a person. New thatched chalets cost P400 single and P550 double. Chris and Jeanette also offer safaris into the Central Kalahari Game Reserve and Tsodilo Hills, catered or non-catered. Tel/fax 659-6959, mobile 7212-0695, e-mail thakadu@botsnet.bw, web www.thakadubushcamp.com.

Closer to town (3.6 km) on the western side of the road is the imposing Khawa Safari Lodge. There is a fancy bar and restaurant, which was empty when I looked in, but the chalets are well appointed and comfortable at P370 single and P420 double. The campsite is a bit sandy and overgrown with weeds and costs P40 a person. Tel 659-7691, e-mail info@khawalodge.bw, web www.khawalodge.co.bw.

The third option is an interesting operation 9 km south of Ghanzi. Turn west off the main road and go 5 km down a farm track to reach a recreated San village. Accommodation is in grass huts and traditional camp-fire food is available in the dining room. There is also an ablution block with hot water and flush toilets. Activities such as witnessing Bushman trance dancing (P600 a person with a minimum of 6) and guided walks are offered, as well as visits to NGOs operating in the area that are involved in the upliftment and empowerment of San communities. The grass huts cost P70 a person or P150 with beds and bedding, while camping with no facilities is P65 a person. Tel 659-7525, e-mail trailblazers@botsnet.bw.

Just 1.5 km north of town and 5 km down a good gravel road is the impressive Tautona Lodge. Situated on a 10 000-ha game farm that plays host to numerous game species, including giraffe, wildebeest, gemsbok and eland, they also boast lions, cheetahs, hyenas and wild dogs in camps. Bush walks and game drives are available. The main complex consists of lofty thatch buildings and the swimming pool is shaded by palm trees. There is a selection of accommodation ranging from standard en-suite rooms at P343 single and P453 double to chalets with a kitchenette for P409 single and P497 double. There is also a campsite situated in the reserve with shady trees, good ablutions and a cosy boma. Furnished en-suite tents are available at P354 double and self-campers pay P62 a person. Tel 659-7499, e-mail tautonalodge@botsnet.bw, web www.tautonalodge.com.

For a truly authentic San experience, drive 24 km north of Ghanzi to the Dqae Qare Game Reserve. Owned and run by the community of D'Kar, this 7500-ha game farm allows the local San people to practise their ancient lifestyle while generating income through eco-tourism. Here the tourist is offered guided bush walks, dancing, storytelling, game drives and a 'Bushman experience' which includes building your hut, sleeping in it and living off the land! For the less adventurous there is comfortable accommodation in a guest house (P450 a person a night, dinner, bed and breakfast) or campsites at P60. Contact them on tel 659-7702, e-mail pngaray@botsnet.bw.

Other amenities

There is a doctor, dentist and pharmacy on weekdays from 08h00–17h30 and Saturdays from 08h00–13h00, tel 659-7644 or mobile 7217-7011. There is also the Delta Pharm for primary health care in Kgosi Sebele Way. The state hospital is in Henry Jankie Avenue, tel 659-6333. Kali Motors at the western end of Henry Jankie Avenue will repair all motor vehicles and offers a 24-hour breakdown service, tel 659-6107 or mobile 7173-9203. For tyres visit Tyre Services in De Graaff Street behind the Shell garage or GFS Tyre Services in Nxabae Way. There is Brooks Auto Parts (tel 7188-6025) just past Delta Pharm in Kgosi Sebele Way and AB Spares behind Ghanzi Tourism. And if your radiator needs repairing, pop in at Horsts Radiator services next to Hollandia Store.

Also next to Hollandia Store is the oldest established butchery in town, or you could buy your meat vacuum packed as well as wors and fish at Artok Butchery behind Gantsi Craft in Henry Jankie Avenue. Artok also employs a woman who grills meat on a fire outside in the yard to sell by the kilo. Upstairs above the Artok Butchery is a bureau de change, or you could use the bank at the Spar supermarket. Gantsi Craft, which is in the main street in front of the butchery, has a fascinating display of Bushman art, crafts and jewellery for sale and is as good as most museums, even if you don't want to buy. Ghanzi Tourism is at the main turn-off into town, opposite Shell, but had nothing to offer when I looked in. Lastly, if you can't find it anywhere else, look for the GFS sign. This stands for Ghanzi Farmers Supplies, and they have all sorts of businesses in town – mechanical, engineering, foodstuff and furniture.

Just on 36 km north-east of Ghanzi on the Maun road is the little San community of D'Kar (see accommodation page 169). The name is derived from mysterious engravings of the letters DK and AR on an old tree nearby. The old gravel road used to pass this way and travellers could support the garage and shop, but now the new tarred highway bypasses D'Kar and the place slumbers. What remains is an interesting old car graveyard with vintage wrecks and an extremely fascinating museum dedicated to the local San people. It is run by the community as Kuru Crafts and is well worth a visit to catch up on the history of the area and purchase some beautiful and authentic Bushman crafts. They can be contacted on tel 659-6308. Learn more about the work being done among the San by various trusts and NGOs by logging on to www.kuru.co.bw.

The Central Kalahari

As the region has become more and more developed and access becomes increasing easy to places that only a decade or two ago were for toughened travellers only, the Central Kalahari

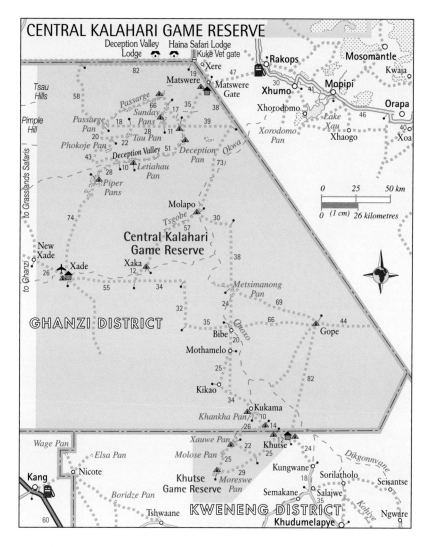

CENTRAL KALAHARI GAME RESERVE

Deception Valley Lodge Haina Safari Lodge
Kuke Vet gate Rakops Mosomantle
Xere 47 Kwaja
82 19 Matswere Gate 30 Mopipi
Matswere Xhumo 41 Orapa
Tsau Hills 58 Xhorodomo Lake Xau 46
Pimple Hill Passarge 66 17 35 38 Xorodomo Pan 40
Passarge Pan 18 Sunday Pans 39 Xhaogo Xoa
20 28 11 Tau Pan
Phokoje Pan 22
43 Deception Valley 51 Deception Pan 73
10 Letiahau Pan Okwa
28 Piper Pans
Molapo
74 Tsgobe 30
57
Central Kalahari Game Reserve 38
New Xade
Xade Xaka 12
26 Metsimanong Pan
55 34 69
32 24 66 44
GHANZI DISTRICT 35 Gope
Bibe 20
Mothamelo
25
82
Kikao
34
Kukama
Khankha Pan 10 14
26 12
Wage Pan Xauwe Pan 22 Khutse 24
Elsa Pan Molose Pan 25 25 Dikgonnvane
Kang Nicote Kungwane Sorilatholo Seisantse
18
Boridze Pan Khutse 29 Salajwe
Game Reserve Moreswe Semakane 35
Pan
60 Tshwaane KWENENG DISTRICT Ngware
Khudumelapye

0   25   50 km
0 (1 cm) 26 kilometres

to Grasslands Safaris
to Ghanzi

Game Reserve (CKGR) remains a place with daunting and wonderful promise. It's about as far off the beaten track as you can get in southern Africa. It is mentioned with a sense of awe by anyone who's been there (or boasting if they are callow), and with an edge of fear by those still planning on doing so. Once as remote as anywhere, but now relatively easy to get to from Maun is Deception Pan. It was made famous by controversial American researchers Mark and Delia Owen, who set up camp here in the early 1980s to study lions. They soon came to words with the hunting community, as well as the government over its plans to resettle the Bushmen of the area. Today you can

ABOVE: One of a very few landmarks in the Central Kalahari Game Reserve.

PREVIOUS: The San community at Grasslands Safari Lodge performs a gemsbok dance at sunset.

stay at Deception Valley Lodge, where they employ San guides and offer various types of interaction with these people (bush lore and cultural).

It lies at the northern edge of the Central Kalahari Game Reserve, beyond which is the drumming emptiness of sparse grassland and sky that our every sense says is desert. It's not, technically speaking, but it may as well be because if you get stranded here best you've got what it takes to get out again. For all its seeming emptiness it is in fact a deceptive land of plenty at certain times. Rain comes in summer storms which can be furious, or some years not come at all. When they do, so does the game. Springbok are the greatest in number, but there are also oryx (gemsbok), blue wildebeest, red hartebeest – and predators. For everyone, the thrill of seeing a huge male

Kalahari lion is a spine-chilling prize (just hearing one at night will give you the shivers, or worse), but there's an equally good chance of seeing cheetah, leopard, jackal – even wild dog, which are highly mobile.

The Central Kalahari Game Reserve is Botswana's largest game reserve at an incredible 52 800 sq km. Declared under the British Protectorate of Bechuanaland in 1961, some years before independence as a sanctuary for the San people of the region, it was meant to allow them to continue their hunter-gatherer lifestyle. At the time there were around 5 000 San living in the reserve, a number which has since dwindled to around 1 000. These people congregate around the only permanent source of water, the borehole at Xade. The official policy is now to move these inhabitants out of the reserve to the village of New Xade, on the western boundary.

The Botswanan government contends it is not fair to other citizens who are not allowed to live in game reserves, and that the San are now abusing their rights by hunting on a commercial scale with trucks and rifles. On the other side, the government, with its partner De Beers, is accused of human rights abuse by wanting to move them off the land because diamond deposits have been found there and the Bushmen might make a claim to that wealth. It's a difficult issue on which to make a judgement call, but it is not my intention in this guide to even try to analyse it any more deeply. If you do visit the area, travel with an open mind and heart and form your own opinion.

Getting there

The Central Kalahari Game Reserve, by nature of its central position, is accessible from many directions. However, with the northern part of the reserve most popular with tourists due to its proximity to the safari centre of Maun, entrance through the Matswere Gate is the preferred route. This gate is easily reached from Rakops, which is on the main tarred route between the southeast and Maun. From the A1 north of Gaborone, turn west at Palapye and travel via Serowe, Letlhakane and Mopipi to Rakops. The signposted turn-off west to the CKGR is about 2 km north of Rakops at S21° 01.970, E24° 22.309.

From Maun, take the tarred road towards Nata east for 81 km and turn off south at Motopi, from where it's another 133 km on reasonable tar to Rakops.

There is fuel and a limited supply of basic foods in Rakops; make sure you are fully topped up before entering the CKGR. From the Rakops turn-off there is a large, dry pan to cross and then the track cuts through the bush with some wallows that could be deep mud in the wet. The newly constructed Matswere Gate (S21° 09.395, E24° 00.415) is reached after 42 km. Bookings and payments are checked here.

If you are approaching the CKGR from the west but want to enter through Matswere Gate, I'd recommend you drive the cutline from the Kuke veterinary gate (on the road between Ghanzi and Maun) to Kuke Corner and then down to Matswere Gate. For this route, travel north out of Ghanzi for 120 km to pass through the Kuke vet gate and turn immediately right at S20° 59.895, E22° 25.377. This reasonably good gravel road is signposted to Toteng, but after 6 km (S20° 59.961, E22° 28.893) turn right onto a sandy track. This track runs arrow-straight for about 140 very lonely kilometres along the veterinary fence until you reach the Kuke Corner Gate. Pass through and turn right in a south-easterly direction along the boundary for 20 km until you reach the Matswere Gate into the CKGR. There is a very comfortable stop along the way at Haina Safari Lodge, 22 km west of Kuke Corner (see details that follow).

The western entrance to the reserve is through the Xade Gate and there are two ways of getting there from Ghanzi (after buying your last supplies of food and fuel). The traditional, direct way is to head south out of Ghanzi for 10 km and then turn south-east at S21° 46.841,

E21° 39.057, and after 160 km of rough road you'll reach the San village of New Xade at the reserve's boundary (S22° 14.660, E22° 47.835). It's another 25 km of very thick sand to Xade Gate where documents are checked.

The other, newer route is becoming more popular as it gives you the opportunity of staying over at the hospitable Grasslands Safaris. To travel this route, head north-east out of Ghanzi (we've already stocked up!) for 37 km to D'Kar where there is a signposted turn-off to the right to Grasslands. It is about 60 km of sandy and stony track to the Grasslands game farm, where I recommend you break your journey (see details that follow). Beyond the farm is a narrow track through the bush for 69 km to the reserve's cutline at S22° 08.203, E22° 47.838 (there is no fence here). Head south along the cleared line for 12 km to reach the 'main' Xade track at S22° 14.660, E22° 47.835. Finally, turn left for the deep sandy 25 km to the official gate.

It is also possible to approach the reserve from Gaborone in the south. Take the good tar road north-west from Gabs for 50 km to Molepolole and then on for another 60 km to Letlhakeng, where the tar ends. This is also your last chance to refuel and you have another 100 km through small villages on sandy tracks to the Khutse Game Scout Camp (S23° 21.380, E24° 36.362).

Khutse Game Reserve

Khutse is a relatively small reserve at 'only' 2600 sq km and was proclaimed in 1971 to preserve the pans, fossil river val-ley system and the wildlife. Two permanent watering points have been established to augment the seasonal pans, and this enables the game to remain in the reserve year round. Gemsbok, springbok, eland, giraffe and ostrich keep the predators such as lion and cheetah well fed and, as to be expected in the Kalahari, the birding is good with many raptors and arid species to be spotted. The 'special' in this area is probably the kori bustard, the world's heaviest flying bird – and fly they can, even if they prefer to stride around on long, thick legs looking for … just about anything to eat. The Afrikaans name *gompou* refers to their love of acacia gum.

The limited road system in the reserve links most of the pans and there are campsites at Moreswe (S23° 33.788, E24° 06.742), Molose (S23° 23.057, E24° 11.173) and Khutse pans (S23° 20.440, E24° 30.238). The roads and campsites just north of Khutse, around Khankha Pan, are technically in the CKGR, but are used by visitors to the Khutse Game Reserve. With no food, fuel or water available in the reserve, it is necessary to be completely self-sufficient and well equipped for any possible emergency.

Getting around in CKGR

The reserve is effectively divided into the more popular northern half and the deep, lonely south where the only facilities are the rustic campsites at Khankha Pan; effectively, though not officially, this is part of Khutse Game Reserve. This southern section has basically only one road, which links Khankha Pan in the south and Xade village in the centre-

More-than-comfortable tented accommodation at Haina Lodge in the Central Kalahari.

west. The 240 km of deep sand to get there will take you all day to drive, and few vehicles go this way. As most of the pans are in the north, most of the game congregates up there, leaving the south even lonelier. Don't tackle this route lightly, be well prepared and travel with at least one other vehicle.

That said, the north is not much easier to get around in. There are more campsites, pans and roads and the area is visited by more tourists, but it is still a harsh and demanding part of the world: all things are relative. If you are entering via Matswere Gate, doing a loop around some of the northern pans and then out the same way again, you'll probably do a circuit taking in Deception Valley, Phokoje Pan, Passarge Valley and Sunday Pans. This way, whether you do it in a clockwise or anticlockwise direction, you'll see the best of what the CKGR can offer.

The main crossroads at the start of this circuit are 37 km from Matswere Gate at (S21° 24.309, E23° 48.205), and south goes to Deception Pan to start your clockwise loop. The track heads first to the four campsites here (S21° 25.705, E23° 47.915) and then through the pan to continue south and west past the campsites in the Letiahau Valley. At S21° 38.389, E23° 25.022 is the turn-off right (north-west) that will loop you back around Deception Pan. To continue straight (south-west) would take you down to Piper Pans and eventually Xade.

The loop road crosses Phokoje Pan where there is another campsite and then San and Tau pans, where you should take the left fork to reach Passarge Pan and waterhole. The crossroads here (S21° 23.930, E23° 15.128) give you the option of turning right to go directly back to Deception Pan along the cutline, or straight across (north) to continue your loop. The loop road heads along Passarge Valley, passing a few campsites and then swings back

south to Leopard Pan. Leopard and Sunday Pans have pleasant campsites and are close to the junction back to Matswere Gate. This loop is about 300 km from the gate and back again and would be a comfortable 3-night jaunt. The direct track south-west, from Matswere via Deception and Piper Pans to Xade and the western boundary of the reserve, is about 240 km and would be a good 2-night visit.

Different organisations control different camps. See page 57 for some clarity.

Where to stay

Outside the reserve

If approaching the CKGR from anywhere along the Kuke veterinary fence, I would recommend you stay at the Haina Safari Lodge or their adjacent Brakah campsite. The turn-off to this 20 000-ha wildlife conservancy (S21° 00.047, E23° 41.073) is 22 km west of the Kuke Corner vet gate along the northern fence of the CKGR. The airy open-plan main lodge has a swimming pool and overlooks a waterhole. Accommodation is in large tents on raised wooden platforms. Furnished with four-poster beds and with en-suite bathrooms that have free-standing Victorian baths, this is the last word in safari luxury (certainly in the Central Kalahari).

With pleasant and knowledgeable staff and excellent food, this isolated lodge is hard to beat for the definitive African safari. Rates are quoted in US$ and range from $205 a person a night in low-season luxury to US$475 in high-season superior luxury. This includes all meals, drinks, activities and laundry. There is also the Brakah campsite for self-drivers with their own camping equipment. Deep in the bush, but with hot water and flush toilets, there are 10 shady spots that cost P50 a vehicle plus P130 a person. Haina offers game drives with regular (almost guaranteed) lion and the occasional leopard sightings. They also offer safaris into the CKGR. Contact them on tel 686-1241, e-mail info@ hainakalaharilodge.com, web www. hainakalaharilodge.com.

The other recommended accommodation outside the reserve is Grasslands Safari Lodge, situated west of the CKGR, between Xade and Ghanzi. To reach Grasslands from Ghanzi, take the road north out of town towards Maun for 37 km to D'Kar and there turn right. Make sure that you have an energetic passenger to open and close

ABOVE: The vastness and solitude of the Central Kalahari affords wild dogs protection in an ideal environment. **OPPOSITE:** Unmistakably a dark-maned Kalahari lion – king of his world.

Before the days of the Trans-Kalahari Highway, Ghanzi and the CKGR could have been the back of the moon. Now Xade Gate into the reserve from Ghanzi is 'just another interesting place'. Almost.

the 13 gates that you pass through on the remaining 60 km to the lodge. But it's well worth the effort (well it was for me, the driver), as this is not only the best and most ideally situated stopover on your way into the CKGR, but also a fascinating destination.

Part of the pioneering De Graaff family's holdings (remember Nelie De Graaff of the Hollandia Store in Ghanzi?), it is very pleasantly and ably run by grand-daughter Neeltjie de Graaff-Bower who is a professional guide and also speaks the local Naro language. The lodge is located on a game farm with adjoining concessions, which border the unfenced CKGR, so there are plenty of animals to spot on game drives, or watch them come to you as the lodge and chalets overlook a floodlit waterhole. The De Graaff family's knowledge of and close connection with the San people enables them to offer fascinating and authentic encounters with the local clan. Guided food-gathering walks, followed by fire making and dancing are some of the activities offered.

Another interesting and admirable endeavour is the Predator Protection Project in which Neeltjie is enthusiastically assisted by her father Willie. The aim is to save the predators that range outside the CKGR and become problems on the neighbouring cattle ranches. They are caught and protected on Grasslands before being relocated and released back into the reserve. This means that there are usually lions, leopards, cheetahs and wild dogs to be seen and heard in large holding camps around the lodge.

Horse safaris are also offered and there is a comfortable campsite with hot water and flush toilets. Accommodation in luxurious chalets varies between P1 800 and P2 000 a person a night, depending on time of year and duration of stay. This includes accommodation, all meals, drinks, laundry, game drives, San dancing and bush walks and even horse riding. There is a separate campsite with hot water and flush toilets that costs P100 excluding activities. Tel 7210-4270, e-mail neeltjie@grasslandlodge.com; web www.grasslandlodge.com.

Kang and the Kgalagadi Trans-frontier Park 19

The lifeline of this region in the south-western part of the country is the Trans-Kalahari Highway. It was conceived some years ago as a shorter, faster route between the Namibian port of Walvis Bay and South Africa's industrial heart of Gauteng. The idea was that Joburg's imports and exports would save time and expense by using this corridor through Botswana. I doubt whether it has proved to be as popular for this as was hoped, but it has certainly made the access to some previously far-out-of-the-way places much easier (for better or for worse).

Subsistence farmers struggle to survive in the red dunes surrounding the Kgalagadi Transfrontier Park, near Bokspits close to where the Nossob River exits the park.

For most travellers heading north from South Africa to Maun, the route through Lobatse and Ghanzi is probably the shortest and quickest. The road is tarred and in good condition and fuel and accommodation are easy to find. But it is a desolate part of the world and you will be glad when you do pull in at Kang.

Kang

It used to be a very important watering hole during the long cattle drives between Ghanzi's cattle ranches and the abattoirs and railhead at Lobatse. Back when the road was a rough, sandy track it made sense to herd the cattle south; now trucks and trailers do the job. At the southern turn-off into Kang is Kang Lodge – good, clean, quiet, no frills, budget accommodation. They offer single en-suite rooms with air-con and TV for P250 and doubles for P350. Tel 651-8050 or 7183-0682. Next door is Harry's Workshop for mechanical and electrical repairs and a 24-hour breakdown service, tel 651-8022 or 7285-5564.

The northern turn-off into town offers a smart BP garage with a Barcelos takeaway and Express Shop. Just south of BP is an Excel garage that also offers 24-hour service, a well-stocked shop and restaurant/bar. In the same complex is the very convenient Kang Ultra Stop Motel. Just off the road for a quick getaway in the morning, they offer en-suite double rooms with coffee-making facilities, TV and air-con for P717 or camping for only P50 a person. They also have double wooden cabins that share ablutions with the campers for P200, but will probably tell you that they're full

(I think they like to reserve them for the truckers). They accept credit cards, debit cards, rands, Namibian dollars and pula – sorry, no cheques, hubcaps or Zim dollars! Tel 651-7294, web www.kangultralodge.com.

Behind the motel is Echo Lodge, a little quieter and off the road, but without the convenience of the motel's restaurant and bar. The comfortable single rooms are P332 and doubles P430. Tel 651-8023, web www.echolodgebw.com. Kang town is a km or so off the main road where you'll find a small supermarket, butchery, bottle store, police station and a health clinic. There is one more accommodation option 25 km north of Kang, away on the western side of the Trans-Kalahari Highway at S23° 30.826, E22° 36.733. Kalahari Rest offers a smart restaurant, bar and pool to complement their chalets, rooms and camping. All hot water is heated by donkey boilers and each chalet has a private front yard with braai area. Double chalets cost P600 a night, double rooms P430 and camping is P75 a person. Tel/fax 651-7004, e-mail bmhe@it.bw, web www.kalaharirest.com.

Kgalagadi Transfrontier Park

This conservation collaboration with South Africa's Kalahari Gemsbok Park has created a new gem in Botswana's already jewel-encrusted wildlife crown, and it is particularly attractive for South Africans. Unlike some of the other game reserves in Botswana, the Kgalagadi Transfrontier Park (KTP) is right on South Africa's doorstep, it has no expensive, luxury lodges aimed primarily at overseas tourists, and it is

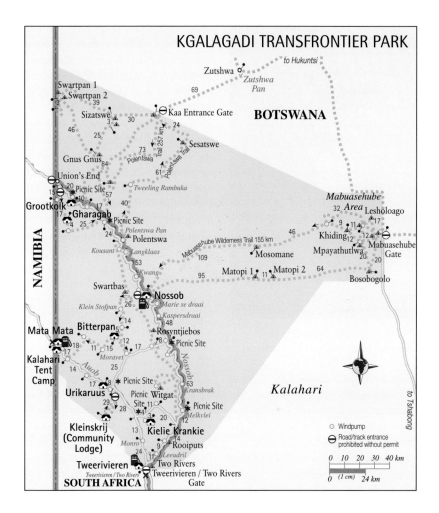

KGALAGADI TRANSFRONTIER PARK

to Hukuntsi

Zutshwa
Zutshwa Pan

BOTSWANA

Swartpan 1
Swartpan 2
69
Kaa Entrance Gate
Sizatswe
30
24
46
25
Sesatswe
73
Polentswa
61
Gnus Gnus
84
Union's End
Picnic Site
Tweeling Rambuka
40
Grootkolk
Gharagab
Picnic Site
Mabuasehube
32 *Area* Lesholoago
9 11
Khiding 12
Mabuasehube
Gate
Mpayathutlwa
20 20
Polentswa Pan
Polentswa
46
Kousant
Langklaas
Mabuasehube Wilderness Trail 155 km
Mosomane
53
109
Kwang
95
Matopi 1 11 Matopi 2 64
Bosobogolo
Swartbas
NAMIBIA
Klein Stofpan 26
Nossob
Marie se draai
14
Kaspersdraai
48
Bitterpan 5
Rosyntjiebos
Mata Mata
8
Picnic Site
18
11 15
12 17
Moravet
Kalahari
Tent
14
25
Camp
17
Picnic Site
63
Urikaruus
Kransbrak
29
Picnic Witgat
Site 11
Picnic Site
28
41
Melkvlei
20
Kleinskrij
(Community
Lodge)
13
Kielie Krankie
Monro
9
Rooiputs
24
Leeudril
Tweerivieren
Two Rivers
Tweerivieren / Two Rivers
Tweerivieren / Two Rivers
SOUTH AFRICA
Gate

Kalahari

○ Windpump
⊖ Road/track entrance
   prohibited without permit

0 10 20 30 40 km

0 (1 cm) 24 km

even cheaper than any of Botswana's other game reserves (I suspect this is to charge the same as on the SA side).

To reach the KTP from South Africa in the south you must cruise up the beautifully smooth and fast R360 from Upington to Askham (where fuel is available) and continue to Andriesvale where you turn right (north). Although this road is being improved and tarred slowly, most of it is still badly corrugated

and potholed for 61 km to the South African entrance gates of the KTP.

The South African and Botswanan authorities have built a grand new combined gateway that straddles the border here and allows access to either side. Here you complete border formalities and then cross the normally dry bed of the Nossob River to reach the Botswanan offices. Another option is to turn into the South African

A family on the Kalahari 4x4 trail sits around a campfire, next to an acacia tree, at full moon.

border post at Bokspits, just north of the Andriesvale turn-off, and book out of SA. Completing the Botswanan formalities is not so simple, as you need to drive 1 km from the SA border post and turn right for another km to reach the Bokspits Community Service Centre. The police station here will stamp your passport and you're in! At least the road north from here to the park on the Bots side is wide, smooth and regularly graded to take you up to the Botswanan offices of the KTP.

From the Trans-Kalahari Highway

To approach the Kgalagadi Transfrontier Park from the Trans-Kalahari Highway, take the Hukuntsi turn-off west from Kang at S23° 40.792, E22° 45.637. This

tarred road is badly potholed for 108 km to the town, which is entered past a big new hospital on your right. The turn-off left to the Mabuasehube section of the KTP is next at S23° 59.995, E21° 47.714 and it is a long, lonely 140 km to the Mabuasehube gate. Whether you are heading down this way or continuing west to enter the park via Kaa gate, make sure you have enough food, fuel and water before leaving Hukuntsi and concentrate – the route can be pretty confusing.

In the town of Hukuntsi you will find Mazagazape Auto Welding and Tyre Works, the Entabeni Guest House, Sefalana Cash and Carry, and a Shell garage. At the end of the main street is a four-way intersection where you'll find a butcher, bottle store and general dealer. Turn right here and after 1 km left at a signpost to Ncojane and Ukwi. A couple of km further, do not take the right turn to Ncojane and Ukwi but carry on straight for a short distance to turn left (follow the faded Zutshwa Camping signs). Where the tar ends at S23° 59.330, E21° 45.420 there is an unlikely looking turn-off down a dirt road to the right. Follow this to cross Mae Pan and continue for 57 km along a wide but rough road to Zutshwa.

You are now in legendary Kalahari dune world. The roads and tracks around Zutshwa are confusing, but just remember to make your way around to the far side of the pan to link up to the direct, short route to Kaa gate. An easier, less sandy, but longer route entails heading 25 km north from Zutshwa first before turning south-west again. But the shorter route is a good test of what's to come

LOST CITY OF THE KALAHARI

A relic, maybe, of a glorious past,
A city once grand and sublime,
Destroyed by earthquake, defaced by blast,
Swept away by the hand of time.

Thus wrote the American adventurer, GA Farini, in 1885 after his claimed discovery of the ruins of an ancient city in the sands of the Kalahari. His claims of finding fluted columns and sculpted rocks were supposed to prove Egyptians had travelled this far south in their search for diamonds and gold. Many expeditions have been mounted since to try and find these mythical ruins, the last as late as 1961, but no evidence of the famous ruins has ever been found. So who was GA Farini? A Coney Island showman who had among his 'exhibits' an Earthman – or Bushman – by the name of Gert Louw.

Gert filled Farini's head with Kalahari stories of great hunting and untold wealth of diamonds and gold. Impressed, Farini mounted an expedition, which included his son Lulu and, of course, Gert. Travelling via London, Farini incredibly organised a meeting between Gert Louw and Queen Victoria. Picture it – the Queen of the British Empire having tea with a Bushman! But the foray into the dry, wild sands of the Kalahari proved to be a big disappointment, although many specimens of flora and fauna were collected and Lulu took photos and sketched. I reckon the American showman had to salvage something out of the trip and conjured up the story and sketches of the ruins to sell to an eager public.

His maps and descriptions put the ruins on the eastern bank of the Nossob River near to present-day Nossob Camp in the Kgalagadi Transfrontier Park. This area is covered daily by hundreds of tourists who now search for game and have long given up looking for old ruins. But back in 1886 these scanty details and sketches were presented in the sensationally successful 'Lost City Exhibition' at Westminster, London. His book, *Through the Kalahari Desert*, as well as the papers he read before the Royal Geographic Society and the Berlin Geographic Society, made him famous – Farini had discovered that a good story was worth more than its weight in gold.

A century later another great storyteller, Sir Laurens van der Post, mounted an expedition to search for the lost city, but again in vain. By this time the ruined stone settlements of the Zimbabwe culture were well known – even if their origins were not as clear as they are now. There are indeed lost cities in the Kalahari, but you'll have to look much further east to find them, around Bulawayo and along the Limpopo River.

in the KTP, so why not take it on? On the far side of the pan (S24° 08.622, E21° 14.731) is a small sign indicating 'Kaa 70' and a narrow, indistinct sand track heading into the bush.

Up and over the dunes you'll go – either an undulating sea of grass or just sand – depending on what rain has fallen. You'll cross pans and spot game for sure, for this is the Kaa Kalahari Concession Area. But be careful, for this is also a hunting area, so don't even think of camping along this track. After 62 km you will reach another track: carry on straight across it and after another 9 km you'll arive at the Kaa gate (S24° 21.500, E20° 37.527). This smart new gate and its adjacent staff housing has recently had solar power and new telephones installed to improve the communication with their bookings office at headquarters.

Another useful route into the Kgalagadi Transfrontier Park has recently reopened at the park's Mata Mata gate. This gate is on the border between Namibia and the South African section of the KTP and had been closed for some years. The re-opening now makes it possible to travel from Namibia, through the park's South African section, into the Botswanan section and out into the rest of Botswana (or in the opposite direction). Just remember to complete border formalities at Twee Rivieren.

Getting around in the park

The park can be divided into three distinct areas: the whole of the South African side, the Swartpan loop in the northern section of the Botswanan side, and the Mabuasehube block in the far east of the Bots side.

The South African side is well sign-posted and navigable by two-wheel-drive vehicles, even those towing cara-vans. The main roads run up and down the mostly dry beds of the Nossob and Auob rivers, with two link roads running across the dunes. Waterholes filled by windmills or solar pumps keep the game watered while the sweet grasses, desert melons and avenues of acacia trees that grow along the river courses keep them fed. Game is plentiful and includes almost all species you would want to see – except elephants (an elephant was seen in the park a few decades back, but it was almost certainly a lost straggler from the north). Birdlife is also abundant with raptors particularly easy to spot.

There are three main, fenced camps – Twee Rivieren, Mata Mata and Nossob – each with a shop selling food, including frozen meat, liquor and fuel. Accommodation is in com-fortable chalets and there is camping available with good, clean, hot-and-cold-running ablutions. There are also 4 unfenced wilderness camps and 2 4×4 trail camps. For more information contact SANParks on tel +27(0)12-428-9111, e-mail reservations@sanparks. org, web www.sanparks.org.

The Swartpan loop on the Botswanan side of the KTP is situated in the far northern corner of the park and is best accessed from the Kaa gate. There is a campsite at Kaa with a long-drop toilet and a Heath-Robinson shower contraption made out of rope, pulley and bucket. All

It doesn't often rain in the Kalahari, but after a good soaking, springbok are programmed to lamb almost immediately. These 'green seasons' are the best time to be there.

other camps on the Botswanan side of the KTP are thus equipped and when booked are for your exclusive use. But what this side of the park lacks in amenities it makes up for with unspoilt, uncrowded wilderness.

When heading away from the Kaa gate, be careful which track you take: the Gemsbok Wilderness 4×4 Trail heads south, the direct route to the Nossob River goes south-west, and the Swartpan loop starts off in a westerly direction. So keep to the right when leaving the gate and travel for 28 km to a T-junction at S24° 14.016, E20° 01.220. You will be able to practise and perfect your sand driving techniques as you cross dunes and pans. You should deflate your tyres to between 1 and 1.2 bar. If there is long grass growing on the *middelmannetjie*, fit a screen or clear the seeds away regularly.

This T-junction is at Sizatswe Pan and marks the start of the loop. There is a campsite here on a dune overlooking the pan and, if you turn left at the intersection to travel clockwise around the loop, there is another camp 3 km down the road overlooking Khandu Pan. A sandy track links the larger pans of the area and travels through typical Kalahari duneveld with varieties of shrubs including guarri, raisin bush and vaalbos, acacia thorn trees and a variety of 'Bushman' grasses.

At 36 km from the T-junction the Gnus Pan campsite marks the most southerly point of the loop, from where the track swings north for another 56 km to reach Swart Pan. There are two campsites in this area which, thankfully, have water taps to wash away the sand and dust. The pan also has a permanent waterhole and is the most reliable place to spot game. There are also a few alternative tracks in the area that should keep you busy for a day or 2. The loop continues in an easterly direction for another 45 km back to the T-junction, from where you must head back to the Kaa gate.

The direct route south-west from Kaa gate to the Nossob River is a pleasant 80 km ride through the dunes to reach the main road at S24° 53.853, E20° 12.080. From there it is another 93 km down a good gravel road to Nossob rest camp on the South African side. Just north of the Nossob camp gate is the turn-off east (S25° 23.823, E20° 35.831) to reach the Mabuasehube section of the KTP. It is a lengthy 160 km of 4×4 driving to reach the campsite at Bosobogolo Pan, then another 26 km in a northerly direction to the Mabuasehube gate. This section of the KTP can also be explored on a loop drive that links the pans in the area. Other than at Bosobogolo, there are also campsites at Mabuasehube,

Mpayathutlwa, Lesholoago and Khiding pans, some of which have permanent waterholes. The road map looks like a pile of spaghetti, so study it and plan your route well.

Another important aspect of the KTP is the wilderness trails that are not open to the casual driver, but must be booked and paid for separately to give you exclusive use of the trail and its campsites. There are 2 in the Botswanan section, of which the Mabuasehube Wilderness Trail is the most southerly. Starting from Malatso Pan in the Mabuasehube section, this 2-day trail runs westward for about 150 km to Nossob camp and can be travelled only in this direction. Along the way (at S25° 07.949, E21° 24.802) is a campsite at Mosomane Pan, which you and your party will have all to yourselves.

The other trail is a 3-day, 2-night circuit that starts 60 km north of Nossob camp at S25° 05.614, E20° 24.553. The Polentswa campsite is just across the dry riverbed and can be used for the night before setting off on the trail. Heading first in a northerly direction, the track passes Tau Pan and then heads deep into the high dunes of this unspoilt desert paradise. After 100 km you reach the first campsite at Sesatswe Pan. On the second day you have another 100 km run, passing the Kaa gate to head back in a south-westerly direction as far as Lang Rambuka campsite. The third day will see you rejoin the main Nossob road at S24° 59.318, E20° 18.983 after 60 km, giving you enough time to drive to Nossob camp (74 km) or Twee Rivieren (235 km). See page 57 for booking details.

For adapted ground squirrels, every one is a Kalahari ground-hog day.

INDEX

All the photographs in this book © Mike Copeland, except the following, courtesy of *Getaway* magazine: CES – Cameron Ewart Smith, DB – David Bristow, DR – David Rogers, DP – Don Pinnock, GS – Gillian Scoble, JF – Justin Fox, JK – Jazz Kushcke, JN – Jackie Nel, PW – Patrick Wagner, RD – Robyn Daly, SR – Scott Ramsay.

Cover: Main photo DP; Right top to bottom, Adrian Bailey, DR, GS; Title page CES; p9 DP; p14 DR; p20 RD; p25 DB; p27 JF; p28 JF; p32/3 Vincent Grafhorst/AfriPics.com; p36 DP; p38 CES; p46 DB; p47 JF; p48/9 JN; p52/3 SR; p54 DR; p56 DB; p58 SR; p60 SR; p63 GS; p71 GS; p79 JF; p83 PW; p85 SR; p89 GS; p93 DB; p96 JF; p99 JF; p112 JN; p113 DR; p119 DB; p120 GS; p122/3 DP; p129 DB; p134 DB; p136 DR; p140 DB; p142 DR; p151 JK; p179 SR; p184 DB; p197 JK; p188 JK.

Other titles in this series...

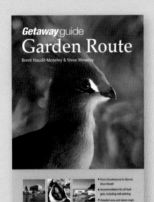

Getaway guide
Garden Route
Brent Naudé-Moseley & Steve Moseley

- From Gouritsmond to Storms River Mouth
- Accommodation for all budgets, including self-catering
- Detailed area and street maps

Getaway guide
Mozambique
Mike Copeland

2nd edition

- Covers the entire country from south to north, including islands
- Street maps and detailed area maps with GPS co-ordinates
- Accommodation for all budgets

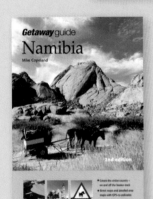

Getaway guide
Namibia
Mike Copeland

2nd edition

- Covers the entire country – on and off the beaten track
- Street maps and detailed area maps with GPS co-ordinates
- Accommodation for all budgets

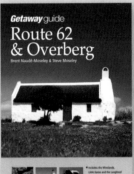

Getaway guide
Route 62 & Overberg
Brent Naudé-Moseley & Steve Moseley

- Includes the Winelands, Little Karoo and the Langkloof
- Accommodation for all budgets, including self-catering
- Detailed area and street maps

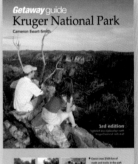

Getaway guide
Kruger National Park
Cameron Ewart-Smith

3rd edition
updated accommodation with Krugerbound rack rack shell

- Covers over 2500 km of roads and tracks in the park
- Gate times and rest camp facilities
- Detailed maps, including maps of rest camps

To purchase any of these guides, or for more information,
contact Sunbird Publishers at tel 021-707-5700,
e-mail enquiries@sunbird.co.za, web www.sunbirdpublishers.co.za

or order on the *Getaway* magazine website
www.getaway.co.za/content/getawayshop/books